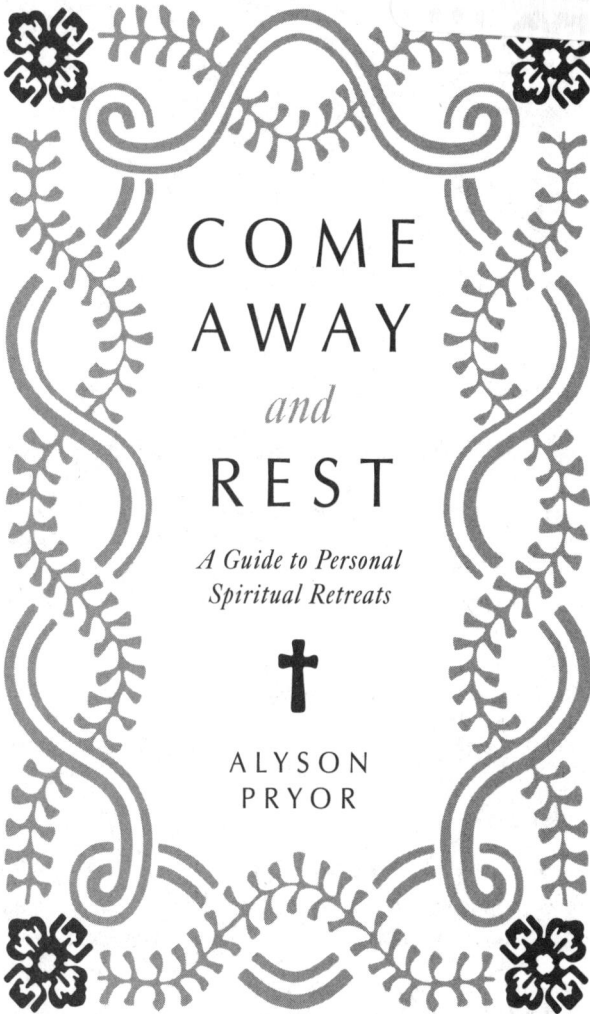

COME
AWAY
and
REST

A Guide to Personal
Spiritual Retreats

✝

ALYSON
PRYOR

ĩvp

An imprint of InterVarsity Press
Downers Grove, Illinois

InterVarsity Press
P.O. Box 1400 | Downers Grove, IL 60515-1426
ivpress.com | email@ivpress.com

InterVarsity Press® is the publishing division of InterVarsity Christian Fellowship/USA®. For more information, visit intervarsity.org.

Scripture quotations, unless otherwise noted, are from The Holy Bible, English Standard Version. ESV© Text Edition: 2016. Copyright © 2001 by Crossway Bibles, a publishing ministry of Good News Publishers. Used by permission. All rights reserved.

While any stories in this book are true, some names and identifying information may have been changed to protect the privacy of individuals.

"Camas Lilies" by Lynn Ungar. Used by permission.

"Walking with Grief" by Andy Raine, *Celtic Daily Prayer Book One*, The Northumbria Community Trust (William Collins, 2015). Used by permission.

The publisher cannot verify the accuracy or functionality of website URLs used in this book beyond the date of publication.

Cover design: Faceout Studio
Interior design: Daniel van Loon
Image: ©CSA-Printstock / DigitalVision Vectors via Getty Images

ISBN 978-1-5140-1122-5 (print) | ISBN 978-1-5140-1123-2 (digital)

Printed in the United States of America ∞

Library of Congress Cataloging-in-Publication Data
Names: Pryor, Alyson Lindsay, 1978- author
Title: Come away and rest : a guide to personal spiritual retreats / Alyson
  Pryor.
Description: Downers Grove, IL : IVP, [2026] | Includes bibliographical
  references.
Identifiers: LCCN 2025027482 (print) | LCCN 2025027483 (ebook) | ISBN
  9781514011225 paperback | ISBN 9781514011232 ebook
Subjects: LCSH: Spiritual retreats
Classification: LCC BV5068.R4 P79 2026 (print) | LCC BV5068.R4 (ebook)
LC record available at https://lccn.loc.gov/2025027482
LC ebook record available at https://lccn.loc.gov/2025027483

33 32 31 30 29 28 27 26 | 12 11 10 9 8 7 6 5 4 3 2 1

✝

FOR MY TEACHERS, COLLEAGUES, STUDENTS,
DIRECTEES, AND FRIENDS AT THE INSTITUTE FOR
SPIRITUAL FORMATION AT BIOLA UNIVERSITY.

You have shepherded my heart in the ways of God and

the practice of rest.

AND TO DREW,

who sent me out with joy.

CONTENTS

THE INVITATION

*Come to me, all you who are weary and
burdened, and I will give you rest.*

Matthew 11:28 NIV

✝

My first personal retreat took place in a convent. The House
of Prayer, a small, Spanish-style home tucked into a resi-
dential neighborhood, housed two nuns in their late eighties
who lived there full-time, Sister Mary and Sister Margaret. Part of their ministry involved letting non-Catholic
strangers like me rent a room for fifteen dollars a day. I began
a small and faltering rhythm of traipsing in once a month,
exhausted, red-eyed, laden with books, slippers, and tea bags.
They would pat my hands and feed me lemon bars they'd
made that morning with lemons from the tree out back.

To say these nuns, and the time spent in their care, saved
my life would not be an overstatement. I began visiting them
shortly after the birth of one of my five children, when a
sudden onslaught of panic attacks left me immobilized. Up
until that point, the only experiences I'd had of retreats were

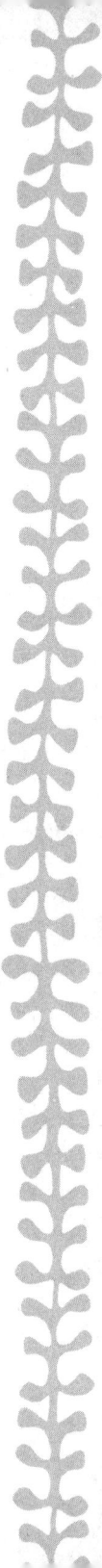

large-scale events the women from my church attended or ones where I was hired as a speaker. My soul was and continues to be filled in a way through those retreats with community, insight, friendship, and laughter. Still, I'd leave with a deep weariness, often more exhausted than when I came. I was yearning for a deeper kind of rest, and the panic attacks took that longing from a whisper to a scream. I cannot say exactly what brought me to the House of Prayer, only that my desperation drove me there. The psalmist writes, "As the deer pants for water, so I long for you, O God" (Ps 42:1 TLB). My thirst drove me to their door like an animal hunting for water.

After a lemon bar, or three, I retreated to my room to settle into my new surroundings. I took in the twin bed and matching nightstand, the small desk, and the crucifix on the wall. I had no idea what to do with myself. I was especially unclear on how much time should be "holy time" and how much was allowed to be "regular time." I was not sure if, now that I had marked off this day as a "retreat," all six hours and forty-five minutes that my kids were in school ought to be devoted to unceasing prayer. I sat on the firm twin bed, wondering if I should take a nap or a hike, read, or pray. I regarded crucified Jesus on the wall across from me. My hands, usually occupied with writing, dishes, ferrying toddlers in and out of their car seats, weighed heavy and useless on my lap. My Bible, so often used for teaching preparation, suddenly felt foreign to me. My thoughts, unaccustomed to silence, clamored for attention. I felt a visceral pull toward my phone and all its distractions. Who was I when I was no longer useful? Who was I without my schedule, my children, my work, my things?

I see in hindsight that I was wrestling with the ramifications of space versus time. Rabbi Abraham Heschel writes,

> The result of our thinginess is our blindness to all reality that fails to identify itself as a thing, as a matter of fact. This is obvious in our understanding of time, which, being thingless and insubstantial, appears to us as if it had no reality. Indeed, we know what to do with space but do not know what to do about time except make it subservient to space. Most of us seem to labor for the sake of things of space. As a result, we suffer from a deeply rooted dread of time and stand aghast when compelled to look into its face.

In our society, opening questions to each other begin: "And what do *you* do?" We have communally agreed that work is superior to rest because in work we communicate our value and importance to ourselves and each other. We measure our lives by what we export into the world, not by what we receive into our souls, as though we could separate the two. Retreating slammed me into the reality of how anchored I was in the *thinginess* of my life. It revealed how I saw myself primarily as one who gets things done—one who teaches, plans, executes, and produces. In aiming to leave *thinginess* behind and enter instead into the realm of sacred time, I found myself on God's turf. I had no trinkets to distract me, no claim on how vital my role was in my own life, just the furious beauty of being face-to-face with God.

Of the many things we might claim that keep us from time away with God, this, I'm convinced, is at the top of the pile. We fear, in the depths of our being, that if we fully surrender ourselves to sacred time, God won't show up. And then, realizing we are utterly alone in the universe, we will slowly dissolve into insanity like Tom Hanks's character in that movie where he gets trapped on a deserted island and becomes best friends with a deflated volleyball. This seemed like a valid possibility only ten minutes into my retreat as I sat on the stiff twin bed.

This fear is real, valid, and surprisingly common. After years of fumbling through my own retreats, friends began to ask me to plan retreats for them. Later, when I became a certified spiritual director, I had even more people willing to show me hidden longings tucked deep inside their souls. They, too, had no idea what to do with time away with God even though they wanted it desperately. They sensed the same call to come away—to leave the *thinginess* of their day-to-day lives—to enter into sacred moments, which they heard bleating for their attention even when they did not know what to give them. They, too, were hunting for fresh water.

When my frame first shadowed the nuns' door, I could have told you only that I came to meet with the living God. The throbbing within me for peace, the desperation for silence, the dehydration from traveling too long without drinking deeply, became too painful to ignore. My soul was in desperate need of rest, the kind only God could provide.

⫸⫸⫸⫷⫷⫷

By the time lunch rolled around at the convent, I had accomplished very little, only reading a few pages in a book I'd brought before drifting off into a two-hour nap. When I woke, I noticed my body felt relaxed, having spent several hours without someone demanding I open a fruit snack or wipe their behind. But I also felt unsettled. I did not know what I was supposed to be doing or if I was retreating the right way. I regarded the crucified Jesus some more. He regarded me.

Once I got hungry enough, I roused myself from the bed and found a homegrown salad waiting for me in the fridge that Sister Margaret had shown me on my introductory tour. I went outside to sit in the sun for lunch. The nuns had a large backyard, with plenty of low benches and paths for walking. They also had an extensive in-ground garden with plump heads of lettuce, shiny stems of beets, and forest-green kale that sprouted up like miniature palm fronds. I noticed the tops of carrots, a hem of string beans, and several more plants I could not name. It was immaculate. I saw, too, the lemon tree next to an avocado tree. Between the two was a bench. I was somehow still tired, so I sat.

Was this enough? I wondered. *Enough to turn my face to the warm sun, to hear the chirp of a bird as it lifted itself from the small birdbath a few feet away, disturbed by my presence? Was it enough to just sit, breathe, and smell the lemon blossoms? Was I enough, sitting here useless, thoughtless, prayerless?* I felt one question hit my soul's bottom, *Did God love me when I rested?*

In a flash of memory, I remembered being newly married—I worked two jobs and my husband worked four—and we were still so poor we only used the internet at the library. One of my jobs was waiting tables at a breakfast place in town. I had a manager there who was the most fastidious rule keeper I have ever met. He repeatedly reiterated the part of the hiring contract that detailed California law on mandatory break periods. I do not know what this man's past trauma was with the legalities of the state of California, but I'll be darned if he didn't know the hot second my four hours were up and I needed a fifteen-minute break. Balancing five eggs Benedicts with a side of waffles on one arm, he would usher me into the break room—my tip lost for good. He would glare at his watch for the vast majority of those unrelaxing fifteen minutes while my fellow employees and I stared off into space, wiping our hands on our aprons, rotating in our plastic chairs to make small talk. He would often tap his foot as if to hurry the break along.

Sitting in the nuns' backyard, I realized I'd made God not into my own image but into the image of this manager. This understanding weighed heavy on my chest that I did not, at my core, believe God wanted rest for me. He might allow it, but in measly bits, like my former manager gave, and only in the hopes of making me more productive for any Important Kingdom Activities I might be called on to do. I had ingested the notion that God wanted to "use" me, and if I was useless, resting, what then? My heart felt so heavy I wondered if it might push through my skin.

"I'm so tired," I offered as a prayer. I pictured Jesus beside me, nodding solemnly. *Yes, you are.* "How do I fix it?" I asked, but the fading image was gone. Still, I felt the sturdy presence. *Yes, yes you are.* I felt a wave of desire, hunger, and thirst for rest and let myself feel it more thoroughly, more dangerously than I ever had before. The wave brought with it anger. Tears pricked at the back of my eyes. "God, why don't you give me more rest? How am I supposed to teach and disciple and serve at church with all these demands at home? I can't keep going. I'm so tired," I said over and over and over.

Once I was done talking, I felt the tears dry on my face. Matthew 11:28-30 (NASB 1995) began to crystallize as my mind pulled at its edges from memory, "Come to Me, all who are weary and heavy-laden, and I will give you rest. Take My yoke ... I am gentle and humble in heart, and YOU WILL FIND REST FOR YOUR SOULS." The call of Jesus, offering me rest, felt like a raindrop falling into a still body of water, the echoes of those words extending, invading some new part of me. I became aware, quite suddenly, that I was no longer on that hard plastic chair in a break room. There was no one making demands on my time. I was on a comfortable, wooden bench, the warm afternoon sun cradling my face. The bird returned to his bath to finish his drink.

My questions percolated, revealing an imaginary divide between secular and sacred time, of what was mine and what was God's. I fixated on how much of my time on retreat (and by proxy, in life) ought to be "holy time," elevating it above "regular time." These questions revealed my ability to quantify and elevate *doing* for God, things I deemed "ministry" or "service," leaving me unable to spiritually quantify time spent watching the sunset, eating pizza, or painting my daughter's nails. They revealed my transactions with a God who gifted me and wanted to use me—an exchange of goods and services—and how that was not at all the same as a relationship with a God who simply wanted to love me.

These questions also revealed my unease with rest: *How do I do this? Why does this matter? What are the parameters?*

But maybe instead of asking *how*, *why*, and *what* questions, I ought to have asked *who* questions. Who is this God who wants rest for us? Who is this God who wants to love us in our uselessness? What does he do, or want to do in rest that he cannot accomplish in our frenzied activity?

I returned to my room, newly energized, and opened my Bible. I found myself in Genesis with a God who rested after six days of work, just to show us the ropes (see Gen 2:2-3). He blessed this time, setting it apart from other kinds of time, naming it *holy*. Paradoxically, in Psalms, he is a God who never slumbers, specifically so he can watch over those who do (see Ps 121:4). Then we reach the Gospels, which show us Jesus frequently seeking out wilderness times of rest. We are told, "Jesus *often* withdrew to lonely places and prayed" (Lk 5:16 NIV, italics mine). The only One whose actions could save the world regarded retreating as vital to his work.

The imagery of Matthew 11, to come to Jesus, is to be with him where he is, and only there will our souls find rest. It is to be so close to him that we are tied to him like one animal tied to another, moving when he moves, pausing when he rests. The invitation is to keep pace with Jesus so that we similarly come away to rest as "often" as possible. If we are honest, many of us would prefer to be released into the fields as autonomous work animals. We would feel more comfortable with the Christian life if it included a GPS location for God's will. But we misunderstand the call on our lives to be primarily people who get things done as opposed to people who stay close to Jesus.

In retreat time, sacred time, we come face-to-face with who we think God to be. Is he demanding, tapping his toe while we sit in the breakroom, waiting impatiently for us to return to our Important Kingdom Activities? Is he distant and aloof? Is he mad? Is he benign like a celestial Santa Claus, with good intentions but perhaps a tad helpless to give our souls the rest they so desperately need? As A. W. Tozer aptly points out, "What comes into our minds when we think about God is the most important thing about us." But what comes to mind for us when we think on God is not nearly as important as what comes to his mind when God thinks about us.

This face-to-face, thinking on him as he thinks on us, is called beholding. And beholding is the only path to transformation, "Now the Lord is the Spirit, and where the Spirit of the Lord is, there is freedom. And we all, with unveiled face, beholding the glory of the Lord, are being transformed into the same image from one degree of glory to another" (2 Cor 3:17-18). Here Scripture offers us an additional image of being yoked to Jesus, an Old Testament image, of humanity face-to-face with God. When we come away with God, we are being changed; the more we look *at* him the more we look *like* him. What I perceived initially as an unexpected consequence of retreat—the terror of being face-to-face with the living God—was actually the plan all along.

A central question of retreat is: *Do I see God as he is?* Retreat offers an invitation to extended beholding, like a honeymoon for lovers or those gauzy, disorienting first days with a newborn, gazing into their bottomless gray eyes full of stars. The Holy Spirit needs time and space to do the deep internal work only he can do. None of this happens immediately, and usually not even quickly.

Whatever we behold transforms us. It forms our souls in a certain way to only and ever behold the finite when eternity is implanted within our hearts (see Eccles 3:11). Distraction is the enemy of the soul, and today's souls are up against more distraction, disengagement, and numb escapism than ever before. If we become what we behold, for the vast majority of us we are becoming whatever is on the screen of our phones. This screen, designed to addict, sparks to life whenever it recognizes our faces. When our eyes and minds and hearts are full of the here and now, the urgent, the popular, the newsworthy—it creates fear and compulsory action. Our culture might assert we are only and ever about what we do—our toil and our turnout. But sacred time away with God "dissolves the artificial urgency of our days," exposing what is most real and true.

Many of us have yet to connect the abundant life Jesus offers with the pace at which he lived. For Jesus, retreating wasn't a pause from his "real life," it was life. He goes before us, showing that face-to-face time alone with God is the very thing our soul is most desperate for. It is the fresh water the animal within us has been hunting. In that fresh, clear pool we see God as he is, and eventually we even begin to see ourselves as we are—if we pause long enough for our rushed work to subside, the pebbles and sand to settle, and our thoughts like so much silt to descend so that we might see clearly.

❋❀❋

The morning after I got home from my retreat, my husband started a forty-eight-hour work shift. I got the school-aged kids out the door, gas in the car, and dog food from the pet store. By 10:30 a.m., my toddler, who had woken up at 5 a.m., was hollering for a nap and I realized I hadn't had a bite to eat all day, never mind luxuries like brushing my teeth. As I hauled my son's squirming body up the stairs for his nap, Jesus' words came to me again: *"Come to Me, all who are weary and heavy-laden, and I will give you rest."* The words washed over me, sharp like salt water, and I pricked at their sting. *Jesus,* I prayed, *how?* I felt angry for having gotten away, the taste of respite turning sour on my tongue.

I cradled my son's head as he thrashed, insisting he was not tired. I tucked the covers around him, gently. As he continued his protest, I lowered the blackout shades in his room with one hand, rubbing his back with the other. His breath slowed, and so did my own. We sat like that for a long time, longer than any day can hold. A thousand memories of coaxing my children into rest stretched out along the horizon of my mind. Love swelled hot and bright in my chest. I love my children and desperately want good for them. I felt the presence of Jesus again, nodding along with me, as my heart cried out for rest. The heat rose to the back of my eyes, filling them with tears. I was loving enough, able enough to give my son rest, to pull the blinds down on his little world, and assure him of my care. I told God that somewhere inside me, I doubted he could do the same. We sat like this, the three of us, for a long time.

When God created the earth, he did so to form it into what his creatures would need: meaningful work and holy rest. The sun hovers above us only two-thirds of the day at most, then God lowers it, a reminder of his love for us within the reality of our limitations. The Judeo-Christian understanding of time is rooted in rest, anchored in nightfall, in the unproductive third of our lives. "There was evening and there was morning . . ." (Gen 1:5). God begins with evening; God begins with rest. Sabbath begins at nightfall, when, for our part, we are vulnerable, useless, and snoring. Eugene Peterson says,

> When it is evening, "I pray the Lord my soul to keep" and drift off into unconsciousness for the next six or eight hours, a state in which I am absolutely nonproductive and have no cash value. The Hebrew evening/morning sequence conditions us to the rhythms of grace. We go to sleep and God begins his work. We wake and are called out to participate in God's creative action. But always grace is previous. Grace is primary. We wake into a world we didn't make, into salvation we didn't earn.

God does not begin with activity but with rest. We, however, think we must check off all the boxes and get all the things done, and only then can we rest. We are, in general, ruthless with ourselves, working ourselves into the ground in the name of Jesus—boring through the earth for that center bull's-eye. Kingdom work, done in his name, we've assumed, is superior to rest.

Jesus showed us otherwise. His longest recorded retreat lasted forty days. Before he ever healed a leper or taught a sermon, we read that Jesus was baptized and then "the Spirit immediately drove him out into the wilderness" for his forty-day retreat (Mk 1:12). The Holy Spirit, not Satan, led Jesus into the desert. Angels attended to him afterward.

The Father's words over Jesus before entering the wilderness give us our best glimpse at the purpose of retreats. "A voice came from heaven, 'You are my beloved Son; with you I am well pleased'" (Mk 1:11). The Father declared Jesus' identity for all to hear: "You are mine" (belonging), "beloved" (loved), and "pleasing" (delightful). These three attributes encompass Jesus' life and ministry, sustaining him for forty days in the wilderness and beyond. Only at the retreat's end was Satan allowed on the scene to challenge these exact areas where God had strengthened him. The reader is left to wonder how the scene might have played out differently if Jesus had refused to come away when the Spirit called, and what he would have drawn on to resist the lies of the enemy.

Jesus was in touch with his soul's deepest needs, retreating to remind himself who and whose he was. It was not enough for him to keep "doing" for the kingdom, silencing his thirst for time away. Jesus retreated before big events or when he had a decision to make (see Lk 6:12-13), when he needed discernment (see Mt 26:39), when he was weary (see Mk 6:31), to reinforce his identity or purpose (see Jn 6:15), when he needed time to process his grief (see Mt 14:10-13), in response to opposition (see Mt 4:1), or for no other reason than to come away for rest and refreshment (see Mk 1:35). "Come away" he said to his disciples, "by yourselves to a desolate place and rest a while" (Mk 6:31). When we retreat, we stay yoked to him, following his example and command. In keeping pace with Jesus, we constantly encounter the world's deepest wounds and needs. Jesus knew what we are still learning: that the more we engage with the world's brokenness, the more we need to come away.

After many years of sitting with people in the state of their souls, I see that we are, as a whole, more desperate for rest than we realize. Our culture fans the flame of burnout. We are overfed yet malnourished, saturated with information yet devoid of the peace gleaned from wisdom. We constantly perform yet fail to make meaning out of our overpacked, overscheduled, overstimulated lives. We follow a Savior who offered us "life to the fullest" (Jn 10:10 CEB), but we cannot locate the abundant life on the shelf, put it in our cart, or find a way to purchase it. Absorbed in the *thinginess* of our lives, we reject holy time as irrelevant. Bound to the things of this world—our demands, our work, and our families— we reap the consequences of continual attachment to the finite. If we let it, retreat exposes our beautiful uselessness, vulnerability, and inability to earn what we most need from God. Holy rest, like salvation, cannot be taken, only received.

Accepting this essential invitation to come away, we receive an offering that has echoed through the ages, "Come, everyone who thirsts, come to the waters; and he who has no money, come, buy and eat!" (Is 55:1). We come to drink living water we cannot buy and the bread of life we cannot purchase, illuminating how we have filled our desires with lesser things that have not satisfied. We come without payment because Jesus paid it all, and he carries the weight of the yoke as we keep pace with him. May we go where he travels and rest when he pauses. May we enter spacious pastures to roam freely, drink deeply, and rest.

Part One

†

PREPARING

THE ELEMENTS

*And he said to them, "Come away by yourselves
to a desolate place and rest a while."*

Mark 6:31

✝

Several elements appear in your retreat experience that deserve a word of explanation. Here I offer some theological backing as to why these elements are vital to your retreat experience: the importance of and natural resistance to solitude, the use of different kinds of prayer, engaging with Scripture, how to order your time, awareness of the body, and the importance of reflection, especially in the form of journaling.

SOLITUDE

If retreating were a math equation, it might read, retreat = rest + solitude + silence. While all three practices prove challenging on their own, solitude is often the most difficult yet most valuable part of the equation. Once, after I'd given a talk about the basics of retreating, a woman approached me with her leatherbound calendar jam-packed with activity. Her opening statement to me included the phrase

"must be nice" about my ability to retreat, and indeed upon opening her calendar, every box was filled to the brim with tiny, precise script. Jabbing at the overfilled boxes, "Where, in here, can I get away by myself?" she demanded of me, as I dismantled the microphone from my ear. She was seemingly unaware that the handwriting in this calendar was her own.

This woman, unable to find time away from all of her commitments, was one of my more honest critics. She let me see her anger, rage, dismay, and jealousy that retreating was out there for the taking, but in her mind, not for her. I have also come across those who were more subtle in their resistance to solitude. They claim retreating is a form of Christian navel-gazing, serenely meditating while the world burns down around us. They pose retreating as an act of selfishness, taking away precious time and resources from Important Kingdom Activities.

Ruth Haley Barton in her book *Invitation to Retreat* explores the term *retreat* in its military context as a purposeful and "strategic withdrawal" of a troop to recalibrate and reassess what is happening on the battlefield. It gives soldiers a different perspective, a bird's-eye view, not just spatially but within. Resting, in the context of solitude, helps us see how close our battle lines are to another person's battle lines, and how enmeshed and messy the boundaries have become. In removing ourselves physically we "pull back from the battle line in our own lives rather than continuing to fight the same battles in the same old ways." We see more clearly from this vantage point which battles are worth fighting and which are not, what is working, and where we are continually spinning our wheels.

Solitude, in the form of a strategic withdrawal from the demands in our lives, sharpens our perspective, illuminating the enemy we ought to fight. We find "our struggle is not against flesh and blood" (Eph 6:12 NIV) as we thought it was. Our enemy is not usually our unruly kids or unsupportive spouses. It is not the careless friend or the bossy coworker. We wage war against the "cosmic powers over this present darkness" (Eph 6:12), a spiritual battle requiring spiritual weapons.

As we mature in God, these battles become more nuanced. If we are not entirely sure what we are called to, and have not taken the time to get clarity from God about the best way to spend our time, we take on all that is good, becoming busier and busier for the kingdom until we burn out. If we do not accept the invitation for time alone with God, we rush headlong through life, assuming we love the same things God loves, and that our end goals are the same. "Our culture supposes that action and accomplishment are better than rest, that doing something—anything—is better than doing nothing. Because of our desire to succeed, to meet the ever-growing expectations, we do not rest. Because we do not rest, we lose our way."

Without times in solitude, we are more prone to lose our way in the world, unable to see ourselves, God, or others clearly. Solitude focuses the lens of our lives, giving us space and time to wonder with God if the contents of our lives are worthy, if our days are fueled by consumption and compulsion or love and freedom. In solitude, we have space to linger with our desires and see if what we are hungry and thirsty for are the things of God or the things of this world. Deepening our roots in solitude helps us choose easily and instinctively that which Jesus might choose. We begin to love what he loves, hate what he hates, seeing with fresh perspective the world around us through the eyes of his kingdom.

When we come away with God, we find our truest selves: beloved children, not robotic engines of production. We declare war every time we enter into holy rest, claiming God can do more in our removal than in our rushed activity. This makes rest subversive, even violent to the kingdom of this world, for in true holy leisure we become more human, more in tune with the image of God within us.

PRAYER

On one trip to the House of Prayer, I met with Sister Mary for spiritual direction. I had not interacted much with Sister Mary, since it was Sister Margaret who gave house tours and took my reservation over the phone. Sister Mary was an enigma: a small, bird-like woman whose stillness I found unnerving. After leading me into her study, she sat like a statue; only her bright eyes moved, shining on me.

She took a breath, slowly. "Would you like to light the candle?" she asked. On the coffee table between us, I saw a vignette of books, a candle, and a small vase of matches. "Oh . . . yes!" I responded, reaching down to strike the match, happy to occupy my fluttering hands. She leaned back in her chair and after another breath said, "And would you like to sing a song?" I sat confused. I was not sure we had the same repertoire.

I fumbled my yes again, and she opened one eye to press *play* on a small black boom box next to her. A lilting voice came on, with violin as accompaniment. I did not know the song. Sister Mary hummed along quietly. When the song was over her gentle face remained serene. She turned her eyes toward me.

There was a long beat of silence.

"Well," I cleared my throat. "Well . . . I've never done spiritual direction before, and, well, I guess I came to see you because I am . . . struggling with something right now." The words, first halting and strained, tumbled out faster. I told her of a difficult relationship I was in, how I didn't know how to set proper boundaries, and my fear of what would happen if I did not but also the fear of what would happen if I did. And didn't Jesus tell us that we ought to take up our cross daily so did that mean dying to things like having boundaries to begin with? I let it all out, grateful to be in the company of someone spiritually elevated enough to solve my problem. I was not completely sure Sister Mary had not fallen asleep in her massive chair. But her eyes opened once I finished.

She replied, "Can I tell you a story?"

"Yes!" I replied, relieved.

"A few months ago I went on a retreat of my own. Normally, I do not hear much from God. But I got a surprise the second morning of this retreat. I woke up early in the morning, and I heard the Lord speak to me." I leaned forward in my chair, anticipating a torrent of holy insight coming my way. In my memory, although most likely not in reality, she paused here for dramatic effect. "He said to me, 'Let me love you.'" And her hands, which had been the only part of her moving, settled onto her lap.

I waited for several moments for the part of the story that pertained to me and my woes. It did not come, and I sensed Sister Mary's contentment, having said all she needed to say. Our session ended. I do not remember who blew out the candle.

I returned to my room down the hall dumbfounded. Was this God's message for me? What did letting him love me have to do with this unsolvable dilemma? Of course, I let God love me. "Of course I let you love me" I even told God directly. And I kept on telling him during the weeks and months after this session. I told him with shoulders hunched, "Obviously I let you love me." I told him when I poured coffee in the morning or sat down to journal my prayers. *Of course I do.*

Agitated, I took it a step further. I provided evidence of how I let God love me. And while the thoughts swirled and a few made their way out of my mouth, I saw a pattern. All of them were about me. I told God about Bible studies I had taught, or times I had devoted to prayer, or moments in the dark at bedtime whispering to my kids God's love for them. On a good day, they might have proven my love for God, but the case I mounted showed little about my ability to receive God's love for me. Midway through prayer one morning I stopped, suddenly aware of my defensiveness and unable to continue. *What would it mean*, I wondered, *to let God love me?*

There is a beautiful moment in the Gospels where the disciples ask Jesus, "Teach us to pray," a request as relevant then as it is now (Lk 11:1). The word *prayer* in Aramaic, a language Jesus spoke, translates to "set a trap." The word *tsela* (Aramaic) or *sla* (ancient Semitic) is the same word those in a hunter-gatherer society would have used to describe laying a trap or a snare. In this visual, God is not one to manipulate or control—a being to whom we present a checklist or make demands. God is a wild thing we seek, who cannot be cajoled into answering our prayers and who is not lured by the bait of our bargaining. This prayer trap, located inside our hearts, remains hidden from the sight of humankind and creatures as the place where we wait patiently to catch God as he passes by. Our posture for prayer, then, is quiet, expectant, watchful, and most importantly, open. Prayer at its core means opening to God's love for us.

Learning to open our hearts to God in this way is a slow and often laborious process, and retreats present a fertile training ground. We are, in general, closed-off creatures, talking constantly, going about our business until something or someone breaks through our consciousness and makes us take notice. On retreat, we have come away and set aside time for God. We then expect God to deliver: a lightning bolt of insight, emotion, or inspiration. He is *God*, after all, it wouldn't kill him to pick up the phone and call once in a while.

On retreat, we receive the invitation to honestly assess our dialogue (prayer) with God and pay attention to what we believe about the activity of our lives. We might find we believe that we are the initiators of conversation with him. Learning to *tsela* opens us to the reality that there is already a heavenly conversation taking place (see Rom 8:34; Heb 7:25). We enter prayer on holy ground even if, like Jacob, we "did not know it" (Gen 28:16).

Christian doctrine holds a theology of prevenient grace, which means not only is God primary but grace is also primary, and nothing begins with us. Before we ever think of coming away with God, before love is implanted in our hearts to seek him, before we come on the scene asking for daily bread, God is already there holding what we most need out to us in love.

SCRIPTURE

Those of us in the Western world experience no lack of rich biblical content. In the history of the Christian faith, the Word of God has never been as accessible, beautifully packaged, or easily digestible as it is right now. We can subscribe to a devotional, request a daily verse delivered to an inbox, or devour any number of well-researched, robust Bible studies on almost any topic imaginable.

This wonderful availability comes with an unfortunate by-product: Scripture has the potential to get swept into the cacophony of information, thoughts, products, inventions, podcasts, terrors, opinions, media, and distractions that inundate us from all sides. Our souls spend the majority of any given day trying to absorb content screaming at us everywhere we look. We are full to the brim with all we must do, all others think, all we could be if we just had the right car, house, spouse, or Bible reading plan. Scripture must squeeze its way into our overpacked lives that often mistake over-saturation with abundance and information with wisdom.

Many retreatants long to interact with God through his Word, knowing that it is often the preferred and primary way God chooses to speak to his people. It is the tool by which God opens our hearts to him, revealing our innermost thoughts and intentions (see Heb 4:12). Many already have an established practice of engaging with Scripture in their work as pastors, seminary students, or serving in full-time ministry, or simply as part of their morning and evening routines. Yet they are often drawn to retreating as a result of burnout in their lives. Prayers, devotions, and practices that used to work no longer do. Their time in the Scriptures, although regular, feels dried up and lifeless. They are noticing that the accessibility of biblical content has not correlated to a rise in holy living and that no amount of information they consume can form their lives in love, toward the direction of Christ and his kingdom. Knowing more has not necessarily produced better lives.

When we engage with Scripture on retreat, it is helpful to get out of our heads and into a lived experience as much as possible, and the Scripture prompts in the retreats reflect that goal. Throughout Scripture God speaks in rich imagery: guiding us into rest in lush meadows, planting the seed of his Word in our heart's soil, causing springs of living water to bubble up within us. God is a flame, a rock, a gush of wind. We often accept these images cerebrally but rarely move any deeper with them.

If we gaze back over the long arc of Scripture's own history, we see not only how well it was preserved but also how beautifully. Looking back at some of the earliest manuscripts, especially those that come out of the medieval Celtic stream of the church, we find their concern was not only in preserving the text but in making it "sing." Their passion for the Word saved it from the Dark Ages surrounding it, and their passion for beauty could not help but be transposed throughout. It was as if when they engaged with Scripture, it demanded to be played with, embellished, and explored in color, texture, and shape.

By contrast, in our culture we seek to understand Scripture better by learning the biblical Greek and Hebrew meanings, participating in inductive Bible studies, and (I'm speaking to myself here) getting multiple degrees from seminaries. But we can also hide behind these tactics to master Scripture, relegating it to our minds, hiding it from our hearts and our souls. So as we enter retreat, we will engage with (perhaps) new ways of being with Scripture: lectio divina, doodling prayers, using watercolors or clay. We will create alongside God and find that we are not only engaging in an artistic endeavor but a worshipful one. We will breathe Scripture in and out of our lungs and let it infiltrate our imaginations. In short, we will see that "our task is not so much to master the text of Scripture as to be mastered by the Source of that text."

Lectio divina. Christians have traditionally adopted lectio divina (divine reading) as a posture of reading the Scriptures *Christianly*, meaning, alongside and through the Holy Spirit. In doing so we listen "with the ear of our heart," pausing between each of three readings to pay attention to how the Holy Spirit might want to help us attend to God's Word. Lectio divina is a four-part exercise (lectio, meditatio, oratio, and contemplatio) guiding the soul into dwelling with God's Word more deeply.

When you encounter a prompt within your retreat to practice lectio divina, before you begin, light a candle if you have one. Ask God to illuminate himself through his word.

Tell God you trust him to guide this time and bring clarity to your soul.

1. **Lectio**—Lectio means "to read," which you will do, reading the passage slowly, considering the invitation that reading Scripture is "encountering God himself or hearing his voice."

2. **Meditatio**—Mediate on this passage of Scripture. You are not looking for insight or trying to figure things out. You are simply receiving this as God's word for you today. Read the passage again slowly, sitting for a few moments to reflect on a word or phrase that "shimmered" or stood out to you. Give yourself as long as you need to do this. Allow God to address you directly through these words.

3. **Oratio**—Respond. Read the passage again, preparing yourself for what you want to say to God or what came to you. Maybe ask God questions about the passage or listen to what he wants to say about it.

4. **Contemplatio**—Rest. Do as you are led. Is God asking you to wait on him, hand something over, or rest more deeply in him? Sit in the loving presence of God—the One who invites you to live in him as he lives in you. End this time of engaging God's Word by thanking him for calling you to come away with him and be with him where he is.

Doodling prayer with Scripture. If you find that your mind wanders or it is difficult to engage with Scripture in this season of your life, try using colors, shapes, and images. Write out the passage of Scripture you are meditating on, and as you go through the four-part movement, allow yourself to doodle and color around the words, making them beautiful. You might pay attention to which words command your attention or "sparkle" more than others, or what colors you are using to represent them. You might find it helpful to place little thought bubbles around the Scripture, writing in your worries and concerns for God to hold for a time, so you can attend to his Word.

Imaginative prayer with Scripture. There will be other places in your retreat where you will see prompts to "imagine" you are in the scene of Scripture provided. Imaginative prayer makes some uncomfortable, fearing that we might veer off what Scripture truly teaches and become entrenched in our own desires and vices. If you are new to or resistant to imaginative prayer, consider that the imagination is part of our minds, and we are called to love God with our whole selves. Any part of ourselves that we refuse to bring to God in prayer, including our imaginations, desires, and longings, remains in the dark, unacknowledged before God and prone to corruption. It is in bringing our imaginations into the light of Christ that he can sanctify them. Consider, too, that when one of the scribes approached Jesus and asked him the greatest commandment, Jesus responded, "Love the Lord your God with all your heart and with all your soul and with all your mind and with all your strength" (Mk 12:30). Those in the crowd listening would have immediately recognized the passage he was quoting (see Deut 6:5), with one noticeable distinction: Jesus' addition of loving God with our minds.

Breath prayer with Scripture. You might also encounter a prompt for "breath prayer," which is as simple as it sounds and a branch of contemplative prayer. Breath prayer is breathing in one portion of Scripture and breathing out another. Or it can be used to meditate on one verse, word, or image. I find breath prayers especially helpful in seasons of grief, loss, disorientation, or when I need to slow my racing mind. Breath prayers remind me that even when I do not know what to pray, God's Spirit, often named *ruakh* or "breath," intercedes on my behalf, groaning within me what I most need to express to God (see Rom 8:26).

Breath prayer can be a foundation to build on other types of contemplative prayer, the most famous of these being the "Jesus Prayer," based on Luke 18:13 and Mark 10:48, "Jesus Christ, Son of David, have mercy on me, a sinner." Meditating on this short passage, while slowly breathing in and out, focuses us on who we are before God (a sinner in need) and who God is (full of mercy and authority). Scripture-based breath prayers are easy enough to memorize and take with us throughout the day, helping us keep God before us as we go about our retreat.

Marjorie Thompson summarizes that in all forms of contemplative prayer, we move from "communicating with God through speech to communing with God through the gaze of love. Words fall away, and the most palpable reality is being present to the lover of our souls." As you engage with Scripture on your retreat, a worthy goal might be to allow it to guide you into contemplative prayer—looking upon God as he looks upon you. Every guide, prompt, and prayer in your retreat is intended to help you come to a place where you can simply *be* with God, trusting he is present with you.

RHYTHMS

The average person moves throughout the hours of their day based on rhythms punctuated by the demands of others, the self, and the almighty clock dinging its alerts in their pockets. One of the best gifts retreat offers is a break from our normally scheduled programming. On retreat we are free to eat when we are hungry and sleep when we are tired. We are free to practice holy dawdling; we can linger in bed for hours with coffee or spend the afternoon lying in the sun. We are free to wonder with God about what we want to do with our day when it is stripped of the schedule and all its demands. This freedom helps us begin to discern what is life-giving and what is draining in our normal day-to-day lives.

Many of us crave healthier rhythms of life, and retreat is a place to play around with what these might be. The earliest Christians understood the need to organize the hours of their day to maximize their experience of God's presence among them. The most famous of these organizers was Saint Benedict, who wrote a rule of life, a guidebook for the household of God—for many the most important text next to the Bible. Benedict's rule was birthed into a culture in crisis in the wake of Rome's decline, the city sacked by barbarians, a world dominated by chaos and fear. The rule is a call to the mindful organization of time—a direct affront (and solution)—to those of us who live distracted, chaotic, and disordered lives.

These monks and the monasteries they established around the world center on the Christian ethic of sacred time. "Monasteries sanctify time, as if to show that all time belongs to

God and our use of time finds meaning only if we do our tasks, both religious and secular, to honor and serve God." To that end, Benedict's rule consisted of three parts: work, study, and prayer, all three dependent on one another. Work and prayer never war against the other as mortal enemies but serve as two legs of a trellis, sturdy planks that hold up one's life. Work without prayer becomes self-centered money making devoid of purpose for the larger world. Prayer without work becomes rote and empty, lacking in passion and deeply self-serving. The earliest Christians, who had to keep food on the table and the lights on, so to speak, understood labor as just as necessary to the formation of the soul as time spent in prayer or study. Gerald Sittser writes, "Such routine creates the conditions for God to do a subtle, deep and transformative work in our souls and in the world."

Every one of us follows a rule of life whether we are aware of it or not. A professor of mine once remarked that we may not formally bow our heads and open our hearts to Steve Jobs every morning, but our phones and eyes and hearts open just the same. We do not intend to waste hours scrolling social media, we do not intend to do many things, but just because we did not set out to do it has little impact on its place in our schedule. The habitual rhythms we live by form a scaffolding that holds up our days whether we put that scaffolding in place intentionally or not. Our paltry response in "managing" time is to squeeze and slice it into smaller and smaller pieces, wringing it out with our hands until it is limp and exhausted. In retreating, we see we might be stewards of time but never owners of it. This stewardship invites us to organize our days around maximizing our delight in God.

We are invited into a kingdom way of living, remembering that Jesus came to give us eternal life. We do not need to fear nor manage the clock—we are eternal.

Just like my own first experience at the House of Prayer, I notice many people who come in for spiritual direction similarly struggle with the expanse of time on retreat. They find themselves wondering how much or what to pray. The prayers and prompts within each retreat are meant to train your soul to pray, to *tsela*, to open to God's love for you— by forming a scaffolding of sacred time to guide your retreat. This will be true whether you choose the six-hour, the twenty-four-hour, or the forty-eight-hour retreat. Often the more depleted we are upon entering retreat, the more this scaffolding must hold up under all that exhaustion. This is to say, there is quite a bit of content offered within each retreat. It is not necessary to do it all for the sake of getting it done. The point is to grow in intimacy with God through prayer. Let the prompts serve you, not the other way around.

The lack of schedule on retreat is a great gift. But combined with a new space, lack of people, and altering of normal routines, retreats, by nature, become both disruptive and disorienting. The daily rhythms (and prompts) provided within the retreats are an attempt to offer some orienting practices. But be flexible here, as you will want to consider a structure for your time in retreat that is sturdy enough to give you a sense of stability, while flexible enough to free you up to maximize your time in holy dawdling.

Each retreat is loosely based on "praying the hours," a common practice in monastic communities. Praying the hours means joining in on an ancient practice with our fellow

Christian siblings. If possible, try a retreat at a monastery that offers this, as praying in a communal (but not social) setting is deeply formative in a different way than a purely solo retreat. A traditional divine office or "hours" is common in Roman Catholicism and traces its roots to Psalm 119:164, "Seven times a day I praise you." They are historically:

- Midnight–3 a.m.—*Matins/Lauds*
- 6 a.m.—*Prime*
- 9 a.m.—*Terce*
- Noon—*Sext*
- 3 p.m.—*None*
- 6 p.m.—*Vespers*
- 9 p.m.—*Compline*

The six-hour retreat guide uses the language of three "sessions" of prayer. All twenty-four- and forty-eight-hour retreats follow the same rhythm of three major sections of prayer bracketed by two minor sections, depending on arrival and departure:

- Upon Waking: Recollection
- 9–12: Morning
- 12–3: Afternoon
- Before or After Dinner: Evening
- Before Sleep: Compline

The three major sections of your retreat are labeled "morning," "afternoon," and "evening." These change within each day and thematically throughout each retreat. After years of retreating, I have found this to be the most helpful rhythm to give me needed freedoms for naps, walks, painting, reading, and staring off into space, yet still anchor me to the rhythm of continually opening to God alongside the natural order of breakfast, lunch, and dinner.

The two minor times of prayer will be the prayer of "recollection" upon waking and "compline" before bed, framing the day at the beginning and the end. These two are similar if not identical across retreats. These small prayers or reflections are intended to open and close the day with God. The prayer of recollection (recalling to our soul who we are in Christ) began with Teresa of Ávila and has morphed over the centuries. I owe my adaptation of this prayer to my dear professor Dr. John Coe at Talbot Seminary. He trains his students to wake every morning with the prayer of recollection. In the years I took his classes, I learned to open to God's love before I even got out of bed in the morning. It remains one of the most sustaining and sweetest practices in my prayer life.

The prayer of recollection I've adapted for the retreat setting has three movements. The first is to train the soul in the vital practice of opening to God, on waking in the morning, using Romans 12:1-2 as a template. It acknowledges that retreating (or any spiritual practice) holds no power to transform the human soul. Transformation is God's work alone, and our only part is to open to him and yield to the work he wants to do. In the language of Romans 12, we are not dead sacrifices, limp and unmoving on the altar. We are a "living sacrifice" (Rom 12:1) constantly wandering off the altar, closing our hearts, forgetting God, and going our own way. This verse reminds us of our ongoing need to return to the altar and open to God's love for us.

The second movement is one of detachment, using Philippians 3:7-8 as a template to mindfully detach from our everyday roles despite their importance to us. This is especially important on retreat because we have intentionally left so much behind. We detach from the finite roles that define us to better attach to God, who holds our eternity. This protects us from creating our own identities as human doings instead of human beings.

The third movement is one of attachment, exploring our most solid reality as beloved children. We pray God's Word back to him, simply and straightforwardly stating what is empirically true about us and our status in the kingdom of God, before moving on with our day. In my experience, retreats can quickly dissolve into handwringing introspection. ("Am I doing this right?" "Is this working?") These prayers are tailored to combat our neuroses by simply stating the facts: *This is who God is; this is who I am . . . here I am; Lord have your way.*

The first major time of prayer will be before or after breakfast (anytime from 9 a.m. to noon, approximately), simply called "morning" prayer. I like to do this early in the morning, leaving a gap of time before lunch to take a walk or do something creative. With each of the major prayer sections, I tend to engage with the material on the earlier end of the spectrum. That way I can go about my retreat, take a hike, rent a kayak, or wander the retreat grounds, and the content has time percolate in my mind and soul, working its way deeper.

At, just before, or after lunch is "afternoon" prayer. It is tailored to deepen and expand what was discussed during the morning session. Know in advance that mornings and afternoons often contain more intense reflection, since I notice I often hit the ground running, especially on my second morning of retreat. Pay attention to what you need and adjust accordingly. The hope is that by "evening" prayer, some of the threads on retreat are beginning to come together. I often do the evening material right after dinner and then have a few hours before compline.

"Compline" is the last prayer of the day for those who pray the liturgical hours all around the world. One of my favorite retreat centers is a Benedictine monastery that prays the hours daily. When they gather for compline prayer, the whole chapel is lit only by candles. The monks give the congregants a final blessing of peace for the night, then exit slowly. The participants wait silently while all the brothers exit, then follow them into the darkness. This is their blessing to us:

> In peace I will lie down and fall asleep, for you alone, O Lord make me dwell in safety. O come and bless the Lord, all you servants of the Lord, who stand by day and night in the house of the Lord. Lift up your hands to the holy place, and bless the Lord. May the all-powerful Lord grant us a restful night and a peaceful end. Amen.

Compline may contain the prayer of *examen*, developed by Saint Ignatius, as a way of observing the details of your day with Jesus. The prayer of examen assesses life-giving moments (consolation) when God felt close, versus draining moments or interactions (desolation) when God felt far away, seeing (without judgment) details otherwise over-looked. The rhythm of compline simply invites God into the day's end as we invited him into its arrival. We will find that our pesky little hearts have wandered off the altar again. God does not need an invitation, as he is already present, but we are retraining our hearts to open to him and to find him in all things.

Whether we come away for a few hours or several days, mindfully ordering our time helps us attend to what God wants to do on retreat. Praying the hours sets us on a rhythm throughout the day to remind ourselves of our true identity and vocation. We have left behind that which seems to be life to us: our accomplishments, purpose, work, and families. We release those identities to grab hold of our true identity as God's child. We empty ourselves of all the ways we try to create, maintain, and prop up ourselves, and then we are more open to receiving "that which is truly life" (1 Tim 6:19) throughout the rest of the day. We cannot hold on to "that which is truly life" if our hands are full of all kinds of other things. This is slow, repetitive training. We train our eyes to see what has become dimmed during the bustle of our every-day lives. We train our ears to hear God's voice above our own, or above the enemy's. We train our hearts, those rusty, creaking orbs, to open to God's love. We need space and time to train ourselves this way. God's voice is not eminently present to us all the time. There has not yet been enough quiet.

EMBODIMENT

Retreats are meant to be one component of the broader rhythm of rest in our lives. Our bodies need rest daily, weekly, monthly, and yearly. We learn to rest in our bodies in an experiential, repeated way, and only then do we begin to reap its benefits.

Kenneth Bailey, in his book on shepherd imagery used throughout Scripture, zooms in on Psalm 23. He says sheep will not eat unless they feel safe and relaxed, knowing they are free from harm. Sheep cannot be trained to sit, like dogs, yet the good shepherd "makes [them] lie down" (Ps 23:2) and leads them by still water. Bailey says, "Sheep will only lie down when they have had plenty to eat, have quenched their thirst and are not threatened by any wild animal or disturbed by biting insects." Rest comes once external bodily needs are regularly met. Retreat must involve bodily rest, relaxing long enough to feel safe with God, safe with silence, and perhaps even safe with ourselves. "The shepherd knows that the sheep need grass, water and tranquility in order to lie down and digest their newly filled stomachs," Bailey says. Just as we do not eat one meal and then never do so again, so, too, we do not rest once. Rest, like eating, is learned, ingrained, absorbed, and practiced in our bodies through routine.

No matter where you are on your journey with God, you can only begin here—within your actual body, your unique experiences, and your specific traumas and joys. There is no other body, no other vehicle by which we are to come to God but our very selves. We relate to God out of our own bodies, our minds, our hearts, our souls. We carry brokenness, pain, trauma, and baggage everywhere we go and most definitely into a retreat. We do not come to any aspect of spiritual formation, retreats included, as blank slates. We are not being spiritually formed as much as *re*-formed, made new, glory to glory. Our bodily realities and experiences matter.

We must practice in our bodies that we are loved apart from what we can accomplish. This cannot be learned in our minds alone; it must be experienced. Rest is bodily ceasing. Solitude is bodily removal from other bodies. Silence is lack of the noise produced by others. Our minds may readily trust God, but our bodies often take longer.

This retraining in our bodies matters more than we might think. We tend to underestimate the disembodied way most of us live. A few seconds into having to wait, whether at the doctor's office or in line at the grocery store, we turn to our phones. We wonder what we could get done, what emails we could answer, what could amuse us during otherwise "wasted" time. The price we pay is that we spend less and less time where we *actually* are. I am not actually in line at the supermarket, I am inside the internet watching a video my sister sent me of angry cats. I am not in the pickup line at my kids' school, I am deleting emails. I am not between meetings at work, I am mentally cataloging my empty pantry and texting my husband a grocery list. I tell myself that I am saving time. If I do these tasks now, then when I am home tonight with my family, I can be more present. Unfortunately, this repeatedly trains us to not be where our two feet are planted and goes deeper and farther than our good intentions. The time we spend "not here" increases rather than decreases.

The book of Revelation gives us imagery of Christ knocking on our heart's door (see Rev 3:20). For those who open to his call, he comes in and dines with them as he did with so many in his earthly ministry. We have been habitually and regularly trained by technology to live disembodied lives, outside ourselves; outside our heart's home. A great gift of retreat might be learning to come home to our bodies in a new way so that we might hear and answer the knock of Christ at our heart's door.

Most of what we call spiritually formational elements of our lives are embodied practices: fasting, feasting, prayer, worship, confession, service, and tithing. We bring our bodies into houses of worship or carry them to the homeless shelter to serve meals. We do these things not only with our wills, minds, and hearts but with our bodies. Because of this, some people find fasting on retreat a helpful vehicle to deepen their prayer life. Some find feasting an integral element of their vacation away with the Lord. Whether you choose to eat delicious, satisfying foods or abstain for greater clarity and devotion, both elements are experienced in your body. Put another way, we do not bring our bodies along on retreats as an afterthought, a sack of skin thrown in the trunk with the rest of our luggage. We experience retreats in and through our bodies, so it is important to consider what they need, how they worship, and what God might have us do with them during our time away. They are the house in which Christ comes to dine with us.

Whatever kind of people we are becoming, we are becoming that way out of habit. By habit and often by necessity, we become enslaved into patterns of living that, even if they did not begin in the body, become housed there. I think of the ways my body was trained by having five kids within nine years. I was on high alert for over a decade:

ears pricked for any loud noise (or silence, which often proved more dangerous), eyes constantly roaming for potentially dangerous situations, muscles tensed and ready for action. Once I noticed my toddler chewing mindlessly in the bathtub, and when I dug around his mouth, I fished out a rusty screw I'd never seen before. I did not sleep for a week after that. Emilie Griffin says, "Since our enslavement occurs most often at the level of habit, it is at the level of habit that our liberation needs to begin." Retreat, practiced repeatedly with God, has the power not only to heal our bodies but to shape and free our souls.

It's normal to need extended hours of sleep or frequent naps on a retreat, especially for those who function at constant high capacity. Traumatic memories may bubble to the surface, along with unwanted sexual thoughts or even a sense of numbness and detachment. When we open up places of intimacy in our hearts, it might become apparent that we have equated intimacy with sex. Vivid dreams, especially sexual in nature, are often reported on retreat. Be aware of these things, but try not to let them become a main focus of your time.

Our bodies give us a wealth of information on retreat, so simply take note, be honest with God in prayer, and get back to your retreat. Remember that you have an enemy of your soul who wants to derail your retreat and get you in a corner wringing your hands about all the ways you have failed or might fail. Remember also that Jesus faced temptation on his retreat. He simply addressed it with God's Word and moved on.

You'll find prompts throughout your retreat to go on a walk/hike or participate in some other embodied—

preferably outdoor—experience. Movement unclenches the body, paving the way for the soul to do the same. God works with what we see: the sunset; what we hear: seagulls; what we feel: the cool water outside the kayak; and what we taste: salt. Sometimes our bodies commune with him before our theological mind has caught up. In retreat, we are trying to connect our minds to our bodies, which allows God to invade our souls—like a Trojan horse—often through our senses.

Retreating reassures our bodies of their inherent worth when we move slowly, enjoying the luxury of hot coffee in a warm bed, a lingering walk in the woods, the cool of water, the crunch of leaves, or the dissolving sand. Retreat must be experienced in the body, and the creative practices incorporated throughout each retreat help integrate what's in the head into the body. Creative practices are about connecting to ourselves and to God, not about being a good artist. If you are visiting a monastery and able to sing the hours in community, embrace that gift. But if not, consider involving song or movement into your daily routine. Care well for your body on retreat: bring cozy socks, new slippers, or your favorite blanket. Let your body lead the way, and you might be surprised where it wants to go. You may cry every day of your retreat or laugh alone in the woods. You may want to dance wildly knowing no one will burst in on you. You may want to sing, even if you've been told you're no good at it.

REFLECTION

Journaling is the best tool I know of to help reflect on experiences. It shows us what we are really thinking, really afraid of, and what we really want. Journaling steps over the barrier of the ego and gets to the good stuff, a behind-the-curtain peek at what is actually going on in our souls. It helps us be more honest in prayer.

At the end of each retreat day, to open compline, there will be no added verses or material. This reflection space offers a time to go back through the day's journal—like someone combing the sand for sea glass or tracing a breadcrumb trail in the forest. It helps us track God's movement through our day. We might find an overall message from our retreat (and it may not have much to do with the themes I presented) that we could've missed. Journaling helps make sense of experiences months or even years later, pulling out insights we may not have seen at the time. It also serves as a road map for the broader journey of rest God is calling you into.

Retreat can be disorienting, especially for those who have not practiced it before. Journaling grounds us in our experience. Even if you only write, "I feel really disoriented," you are naming and mirroring your experience back to yourself. This helps ground you in the moment and note how you were feeling (and when) for your post-retreat debrief.

Research shows that free writing for fifteen to twenty minutes a day, connecting a traumatic experience to how a person felt about it, had outcomes similar to therapy. Writing in this way often serves to unburden us. Knowing no one will read what you have written might free you up to confess, release, and generally be more honest with God. It reminds our souls that "prayer is not a place to be good, it is a place to be honest."

Questions have the power to disarm and get us into deeper places than answers do, which might be why Jesus was so fond of asking them. Be sure to linger with prompts that seem to hit a chord in you (including the chord of resistance), spending as much time as you want on each one, instead of trying to journal the same amount for each section. Keep in mind that the questions are tailored throughout the retreats as a ladder, taking you deeper, step by step, into what God has for you. Do your best to engage with them, remembering that journaling is the best way to get everything out of these questions. God has his own agenda for your time away, so trust the Holy Spirit's leading on where to dive deep and what to leave to address later.

PREPARATION GUIDE

✝

CAMAS LILIES

LYNN UNGAR

Consider the lilies of the field,
the blue banks of camas opening
into acres of sky along the road.
Would the longing to lie down
and be washed by that beauty
abate if you knew their usefulness,
how the natives ground their bulbs
for flour, how the settlers' hogs
uprooted them, grunting in gleeful
oblivion as the flowers fell?
And you—what of your rushed
and useful life? Imagine setting it all down—
papers, plans, appointments, everything—
leaving only a note: "Gone
to the fields to be lovely. Be back
when I'm through with blooming."
Even now, unneeded and uneaten,
the camas lilies gaze out above the grass

from their tender blue eyes.
Even in sleep your life will shine.
Make no mistake. Of course
your work will always matter.
Yet Solomon in all his glory
was not arrayed like one of these.

There are many tactical aspects to prepare for your retreat, but none is as vital as the will to lay it all down, leaving only a note, "Gone to the fields to be lovely." At its heart, this is what retreat is—going to the fields to be lovely and be loved. All determined preparation must have this in mind.

From all accounts, it seems as if Jesus approached re-treating this way—up and leaving those he was with, pre-sumably with no warning. I like this visual of him, quietly gathering his belongings midconversation, then wandering off into the wilderness for days at a time. May we emulate his spirit of not seeking validation nor a stamp of approval for our time away. Jesus simply went into the fields to be lovely and be loved.

Most of us, however, will need more than a sticky note to alert our loved ones or employers to our departure. In fact, the better we plan for our time away, the more completely we can let go of our normal day-to-day responsibilities. Eugene Peterson says, "The trick, of course, is to get to the calendar before anyone else does. . . . It is the one thing everyone in our society accepts without cavil as authoritative. . . . I mark out times for prayer, for reading, for leisure, for the silence and solitude out of which creative work—prayer, preaching, and listening—can issue."

Make peace with the fact that no one will do this for you, and just because it is difficult to carve out a time for solitude does not make it unworthy, or worse, unchristian. We all walk the tightrope between human labor and divine grace. God never forces us to come away. He does not bang down the door of our heart but knocks gently. And as far as I have experienced, he neither divinely makes a reservation for me at a monastery nor procures snacks for the drive. We "strive to enter that rest" (Heb 4:11); retreating is not devoid of effort, planning, and intent. Dallas Willard famously said, "Grace is not opposed to effort but to earning," solidifying the reality that we are not earning a thing by heeding God's call to come away with him. Yet it often requires effort on our part to make it happen.

CHOOSING A RETREAT

When someone says "retreat," different images come to mind. For some, the only framework they have is a corporate retreat, which takes place in a different setting than normal work and often involves more time "on" than "off" with their employer and coworkers. Some think of large-scale venues where an author or speaker is hired to inspire the crowd, which while insightful, often prove more exhausting than restorative. Some may think of something from the Eastern tradition, which seems otherworldly and unattainable.

The kind of retreat modeled after the life and teachings of Jesus is one of rest and intimacy with God. We know Jesus usually retreated alone, but occasionally he was with his disciples. We know it involved prayer and silence. We know it was set apart from but deeply affected by his active ministry.

We know the goal was communion with the Father. Apart from those things, we know very little.

Part of your preparation time will be devoted to prayer and discernment about how long to get away and what retreat to choose. Linger with these questions and prompts for as long as you need to. Pay attention to what comes up in your heart as you address what you most want out of a retreat. Get curious about the retreats that appeal to you as much as the ones that repel or scare you. Don't assume just because you have a looming deadline that the discernment retreat is what is right for you. As you will find with each of the retreats, the impetus that is calling you there is the beginning of the journey, not the end. God often has a different agenda than we do for our time away together, but the end is always the same—experiencing deeper rest with God.

Of the five retreats, "For One in Need of Rest" is the most general, designed for those who are new to retreating or who do not feel particularly drawn to another topic. This is also the only retreat with six-hour, twenty-four-hour, and forty-eight-hour versions to help the curiously hesitant ease into a practice of retreating. The six- and twenty-four-hour retreats begin in the morning, but all forty-eight-hour retreats begin and end at midday to accommodate most locations' check-in and checkout schedules, and to plan for travel. "For One Who Is Weary" was written for those who have become aware of a deep level of fatigue or burnout in their vocation, home life, and even spiritual walk. The "For a Time of Transition" retreat is designed for those who find themselves in the wilderness at one of many turning points in life—whether they chose the change of circumstance or not—with hope to navigate a faithful path forward. "For One Who Is Grieving" is better suited for those who are not in the early stages of traumatic loss but rather later when they need to unpack levels of healing despite the time that has passed or the nature of the grief. "For One in Need of Discernment" explores movements behind decision-making and how God is growing retreatants to be good choosers capable of co-laboring with him in the work he has given us to do in the world.

NUTS AND BOLTS

This section includes practicalities to consider as you prepare to come away. It assumes the retreat center or lodging is away from home, with checking in for overnight in the afternoon and checkouts in the late morning, as your forty-eight-hour retreat guide follows that rhythm. The day retreat begins in the morning and ends in late afternoon to accommodate children's school schedules or a monthly half-day retreat churches are increasingly offering to their employees.

Plan ahead. Consider a day retreat (using the six-hour guide) if you are a nursing mother or a full-time caregiver to small children. It is better to do monthly or quarterly day retreats, fully immersed, rather than try to get away for a weekend, only to be checking in constantly. The aim is fully focused time with God, so whatever time frame in which you can accomplish that kind of detachment is ideal. Retreats are meant to be one aspect of a greater rhythm of holy leisure in our life in God, so start with something accessible that you can build on.

Role of community. Consider journeying with others in silence if you have never done a solitude retreat before. There are monasteries and conference centers that host the retreatant, offering not only lodging but food, grounds for walking, and sometimes corporate prayer. Receiving, in silence, a meal prepared is a humbling and healing event, especially for those in a caregiving or serving role at home. As my kids' preschool teacher often said, "You get what you get and you don't get upset." Submitting oneself to the (often vegetarian) diet of monks is a practice in of itself, yielding to what they serve and when they serve it. Likewise, praying the hours in community lets you have controlled solitude. You can retreat to your private room, but the setting is among the monks and other retreatants. I have found that corporate prayer, often sung over me, is incredibly healing, especially in seasons when my community life at home has been fractured or lacking.

Mental and physical health. If you are currently struggling with your mental health, consult with your therapist before committing to time in solitude and silence. This is also true for those in the early stages of a profound loss. If you have physical health needs, make sure to integrate those as you plan your retreat and its location, allowing for private bathroom facilities, wheelchair accessibility, and the like.

Support. Use part of your preparation time to find a spiritual director or trusted friend to engage in this retreat content with you. Debriefing your retreat experience with a spiritual director, pastor, or trusted friend helps you make sense of what happened on your retreat as part of the larger movements of

God in your life. Ask one or more trusted friends to pray over your time away—this is essential. God has an agenda for your time away. So does the enemy of your soul.

Think through how to delegate emergency situations to others in your absence. Let your family and friends know you will be unreachable and keep your phone in airplane mode, turned off, or locked in the trunk of your car.

Environment. The majority of us move between two options in our everyday environment: home and work. The goal for a retreat is to find a third option: a place where there are no demands on your attention, no laundry to fold, and no deadlines to meet. The ideal environment for a retreat is one of silence and solitude. In retreat, we aim to quiet the soul. Unfortunately, this leaves room for all our emotional baggage to bubble to the surface and demand our attention. It is very tempting to want to escape the silence if it becomes overwhelming or when thoughts clamor for attention. This is normal and expected. We aim to sit with God in the quiet and not simply fill the silence with other noises or distractions. Try to pick a location without televisions in the rooms and minimal outside distractions. Consider in advance what kind of environment sparks your curiosity or relaxes your senses. Having access to the outdoors is vital for many on retreat. For this, and other reasons, hotels are usually last on the list of spaces conducive to retreating. Consider an Airbnb, a friend's unused cabin or backhouse, or if you're feeling adventurous (and you've done it before), reserve a camping spot. You might be surprised by how many monasteries allow outsiders to rent a room for the day or use their grounds for free. There are ways to get creative if finances are tight. Ask around for a friend or friend of a friend to swap houses or apartments with someone who also wants to retreat. Put feelers out to housesit for those going out of town. There are often low-cost venues that host retreatants if you are willing to bring your own food and linens.

What to pack. It will be essential to bring a Bible and a journal to record your thoughts, prayers, and experiences. I also pack a candle, new cozy socks, comfortable clothes, hiking or walking shoes, water shoes, slippers, and a bathing suit. Each retreat has prompts for creative expression to help get your theology from your head into your body and soul. I always bring paper, watercolors, fancy pens, markers, and perhaps some modeling clay or Play-Doh. This is not about creating "good" art but about allowing God to engage with us in a new and embodied way. If you have ways of expressing yourself creatively or want to try something new, be sure to pack those supplies as well.

Personal needs. Before going on retreat, reflect on what in your regular day is life-giving and what is burdensome or challenging. A caregiver for young children might find it beneficial to go to a retreat location where all meals and linens are provided. Someone who works long hours in an office might choose a location with lots of hiking trails or a view of mountains. A retiree who is alone all day might find praying the hours in community refreshing. A pastor who works with words and Scripture all day may find it freeing to go camping on the beach, bringing along a surfboard. Ask God how he might want to meet with you in this time to bring rest and refreshment within the context of your unique personality, work, and life stage.

Many of us need extra sleep on retreat, so plan to go to bed early, take naps, or let yourself sleep as late as you need to. Do not pack your retreat full of activities. Pack an eye mask, noise-canceling machine, and maybe a natural sleep aid, if you've gone too long without solid rest and know you will have a hard time sleeping in a new location. Plan healthy meals in advance to freeze and bring, if you are not going to a retreat center with meals included. At the same time, try to accept the limitations of your location as a gift from God. Notice what you need, but also try to accept any unmet needs (i.e., the food offered is not to your liking) as an invitation to keep your focus on God and more deeply surrender to what he is doing on your retreat.

Preparation. Familiarize yourself with the retreat you plan to use. Sit with the following questions, returning to them as often as is helpful in the weeks leading up to your retreat.

PREPARING YOUR SOUL

✝

Along with preparing our families and workplaces for our departure, we benefit from preparing the soil of our soul. In the guided questions below, you will be encouraged to imagine longer periods of rest than perhaps you are able to undertake now, to help inform the broader rhythm of rest you might want to integrate into your life. Allow these questions to percolate in your soul during the days or weeks leading up to your retreat. Use them to guide conversations with your pastor, trusted friend, or spiritual director. Journal your answers and return to the ones that spark your interest. The answers may prove useful before, during, or after your time away.

1. What is your relationship with silence? (Consider how it was modeled in your childhood home, if it was ever used negatively against you, how you cope with silence in intimate relationships, or times you avoid silence in your daily life, especially when you are alone). Talk honestly with God about any fears you have about this time away in silence.

2. What limitations are you hitting in your life right now? In what areas do you feel like you are at the end of your rope?

3. What do you most need right now? Try to list all that your soul needs that you become aware of.

4. What are you longing for? (A few hints: What websites are you visiting? What is in your online shopping cart? What commonalities are there and what insights might this give you about your soul's true hunger and thirst?)

5. What feels particularly heavy in your life right now? Think through relationships, obligations at home and at work, and the mental pileup of things undone.

6. If you had no demands on your time, energy, finances, and the like, what would you most want to do? Where would you want to go? Pray and ask God to help you find the deeper longings embedded in these desires.

7. When your mind wanders in prayer (*when*, not *if*) where does it go? Pay attention to this in your prayer life over several days. Which themes or commonalities are worth exploring?

8. Some instructions on (sabbath) rest are to "bear no burden" (Jer 17:21 NKJV) but also to strive "to enter God's rest" (Heb 4:11 NCV). In preparing for your retreat, what might you need to lay down in surrender and what might you want to pick up and receive?

9. What most convinces you of your need for rest? How do you know now is the time to step away from your everyday life for a time of solitude?

10. For how much time can you realistically plan to come away?

11. How will your current needs affect which retreat you choose? Which retreat are you drawn to? Are there any you are resistant to? Ask God which retreat he would have you begin with.

12. Think critically about your goals for your retreat. Often these are subconscious, a hidden hope that you will get something from your time away, and if you do not, it will have been a waste or unsuccessful. Ask God how to attribute meaning to your time away. What do you most hope for? What do you think God most hopes for in your time alone together?

13. God what I most want to tell you right now is ...

Part Two

✝

THE

RETREATS

ARRIVAL GUIDE

✝

I suggest using this arrival guide each time you enter a retreat. It prepares your soul and body to enter a new space and reinforces your intention to come away with God. You are claiming this space and time as sacred unto God, despite what may have happened here previously and despite how you find yourself entering retreat. It is a line in the sand that dedicates this space as holy, set apart for God and his purposes, and helps you affirm your commitment and desire to meet with him here.

ARRIVAL SCRIPTURE—PSALM 62:1

For God alone my soul waits in silence;
from him comes my salvation.

ARRIVAL PRAYER

Dear God, your goodness and mercy pursue me every day of my life (see Ps 23:6). I pause now and let it catch up to me. I receive this time of rest as a gift from you. Thank you for calling me to come away with you by preparing this

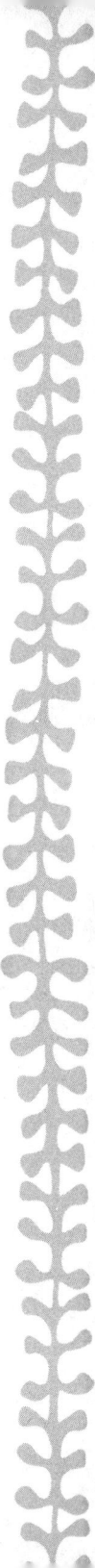

time and place for my retreat. I trust you will meet me here and do more in my resting than I can in my striving. I pray in the name of Jesus that you would bind all evil from this place. May your kingdom reign here in this space and in my heart. I want your will to be my will and your will to be done. Guard this time. Watch over those I've left behind; watch over my comings and goings. Amen.

REFLECTION

Take a few moments in silence, here at the beginning of your retreat, by reflecting on what you need to surrender to fully give yourself to the retreat experience. Take out a sheet of paper and write down anything that is taking up space in your soul. Take a moment to swiftly address any issues that cannot wait until you return home. Return to this paper throughout your retreat to jot down any worries or nagging tasks, envisioning yourself handing them over to God's watchful care until your retreat is over.

Questions for Journaling

- What do you need to surrender to fully enter into this time away with God? (Consider tangible responsibilities like deadlines, along with relational roles, conflicts, and stressors.)
- How does it feel to entrust your responsibilities, worries, relationships, and cares to God to hold during your retreat?
- What else is keeping you from being fully present to God during this time?
- God, what I most hope for in this time away with you is . . .

Settle into your space. While unpacking your belongings, set aside a place to pray. Keep your Bible there, so it is accessible to you when the Lord speaks to you through his Word. Consider bringing items from the outdoors into this space—a rock, leaf, or sea glass—to ground you in your location. Bring out your candle if you brought one, whose light serves as a reminder of Christ's presence with you.

Take a walk, or a nap. Do this especially if your journey was long. This signals to your body that this time is about resting in God, not doing for God. Recall that Jesus napped in times of busyness and even crisis (see Mk 4:38). As you continue to familiarize yourself with the location and give your body a sense of orientation, meditate on God's action that brought you to where you are now. "No one can come to me unless the Father who sent me draws him" (Jn 6:44). Thank God for drawing you away to be with him.

6

FOR ONE IN NEED OF REST

Note: This is the only retreat with six-, twenty-four,
and forty-eight-hour versions.

✝

My earliest attempts at rest looked something like this: My
husband would arrive home from a shift at work, I would
thrust the baby at him, drive to the nearest big box store,
get an iced coffee, and roam the aisles zombie-like, filling
my cart.

Or.

Beginning to take seriously the invitation to sabbath, I'd
block off the day from all activities but church. Once home,
the kids would meander to the backyard to play, the baby
would go down for a nap, and I would stare at the ceiling
for about half an hour before opening my phone or computer, looking for a show to watch or a new blouse to buy
or a house we could never afford to rent on the beach for
summer vacation.

Accepting God's invitation to rest, retreats included,
means leaving the shallow end of our soul's pond and

venturing into deeper waters. Here, we are immediately confronted with all the tactics, habits, and patterns we have used to keep ourselves afloat. Some of us will see how well trained we have become by the consumeristic culture in whose waters we normally swim. For others, we will be confronted with the treasures of our hearts, as we notice what we give our attention to that is something or someone other than God. Moving from the shallows to the deep means the daily façades we normally rely on no longer hold us up. In rest we are given valuable insights into what life preservers we reach for.

This retreat examines our attachments so we might see more clearly the scaffolding that gives our lives shape—or put in spiritual terms, our rule of life. Even if you have not sat down and formally put pen to paper, there are things you do every day—practices, habits, and routines—that make up your life. Even after years of practicing a rhythm of retreating, I find it helpful to reexamine these life preservers, these attachments, and consider with God if I am living the life Christ wants to live through me.

As we move into the deep end, we leave worldly distractions in their place in the shallows and give God our most precious commodity: our attention. *Attention economics* treats human attention as a way to make a profit. "Attention is treated as a resource—a person has only so much of it." The term was first coined by economist Herbert A. Simon who said, "In an information-rich world, the wealth of information means a dearth of something else: a scarcity of whatever it is that information consumes. What information consumes is rather obvious: it consumes the attention of its recipients. Hence a wealth of information creates a poverty of attention." I am not sure if any phrase encapsulates the modern condition better than "poverty of attention."

Time and attention are outpacing other forms of currency and are fast becoming our most precious commodities. We do not often assess how we are spending these commodities and whether that lines up with what we value and what we want. One aim of this retreat is to be generous with our time and attention toward God, the two things most often atrophied in our spiritual lives. We may be generous to God in our tithing, church attendance, or our willingness to serve. But are we generous in our attention toward God himself?

When we enter into silence and solitude, we answer our soul's cry for rest and refreshment. "For thus said the LORD God, the Holy One of Israel, 'In returning and rest you shall be saved; in quietness and in trust shall be your strength'" (Is 30:15). Retreating does not procure our salvation, but it can rescue us from the "tyranny of the urgent," as it separates us for a time from the demands of our lives. In heeding God's call to return and rest, we pause our efforts and cease our striving, turning our focus toward God. Our souls yearn for this deep water more than we let ourselves realize. We thirst for uninterrupted time with the lover of our souls, for the serenity that comes after many hours of deep and restorative silence stacked one upon the other, settling and quieting our spirit. As unmooring as it may feel at first, giving God our attention on retreat trains us to float in the deep end instead of floundering on the shoreline.

Accepting the invitation to move out into the deep with God offers us a different point of view than our normal lives allow. We get a bird's-eye view as we tread out into deeper waters, not just spatially but within. Coming away to assess the situation of our lives is not unlike Jesus, who pushed boats out into the water to better address the crowds on the shore. In this retreat, we detach from our world with all its joys, burdens, and distractions to more fully attach to God in the deep places of our souls. From this vantage point, we might see more clearly what is exhausting us or what is unexpectedly holding us up.

Begin by reviewing chapter five, the "Arrival Guide."

....

SESSION ONE—MORNING OR UPON ARRIVAL

The Heart's Treasures

OPENING SCRIPTURE—MATTHEW 6:21

Where your treasure is, there your heart will be also.

OPENING PRAYER

God, here I am. I present myself to you and open my heart to you and what you will do on this retreat. Be with me as I assess where my heart and treasures lie, and let me be compassionate with myself, remembering you are always compassionate with me. Amen.

REFLECTION

Jesus was fully attached to his Father, giving him his full focus and attention. Jesus did not have any disordered attachments to anything or anyone. He says of himself, "Truly, I say to you, the Son can do nothing of his own accord, but only what he sees the Father doing" (Jn 5:19). His every action was a response to what he saw his Father doing first.

Jesus stresses to his disciples the importance of being rightly attached to him, and therefore his Father as well. "Abide in me, and I in you" (Jn 15:4) was among his final instructions, highlighting the importance of staying attached, connected, and dwelling in him. Yet even the disciples, those who heard Jesus' words at this moment, did not abide perfectly. Thomas Green describes how the disciples' attachment to the things of the world clouded and blocked their ability to be fully open to what God was doing in their midst:

> Their attachments—to honor, to wealth, to security, to life itself—complicated and confused their discernment. ... They discerned but not infallibly or unerringly. Jesus' discernment was unerring because he was totally open to the Spirit. ... But most of our lives are like Peter. He loved Jesus; he loved God. ... [H]e loved "God and" rather than "God only." He truly wanted God's will. But he wanted other things too. And these other wants, which the saints call disordered attachments when they prevent us from floating free in the sea of God, blocked his discernment of Jesus.

In this retreat we will gently take stock of our heart's attachments. Take out paper and a pen as you prepare to open your heart to God. Take a few deep breaths and simply let your mind rest.

Read Matthew 6:19-21, picturing Jesus addressing you personally through these words. As you imagine yourself in this scene, see where your heart wants to go. Spend five to ten minutes in silence dwelling on Jesus' words.

Questions for Journaling

- ⌇ What is bubbling up; rising to the surface?
- ⌇ Where does your soul want to go when it doesn't have somewhere else to be, when there are no demands on its time or attention? Be honest here.
- ⌇ What does your soul want to tell you? What is it showing you?

✑ Do your best not to make judgments. You are honestly assessing your heart's treasures. This information is good and useful. Take note of what feels important to you, what you're concerned about, and where your mind wanders.

✑ Where do you feel "totally open to the [Holy] Spirit" and what he is doing in your life?

✑ What is preventing you from "floating free in the sea of God"? What attachments do you carry that might be tethering you to something other than God?

CLOSING PRAYER

Thank you, God, that your knowledge of me is complete, unerring, and unending. Give me the wisdom and clarity I need to explore the landscape of my soul and all the treasure within it. Search me, O God, and know my heart. Test me and know my anxious thoughts. See if there is any offensive, hurtful, or grievous way within me and lead me in your way everlasting (see Ps 139). Let me see what you want me to see. Protect, seal, and hem in my heart as you promise to do. Amen.

⟩⟩⟩⟨⟨⟨

Close this first session by thanking God for his complete knowledge of and total love for you. Consider meditating on all of Psalm 139 as you go about your morning, taking a walk or resting, letting your body lead the way before diving into session two. As you go, continue to pay attention to what is bubbling up within you, and share it with the Lord as one friend speaks to another.

SESSION TWO—LATE MORNING OR MIDDAY

Taking Inventory

OPENING SCRIPTURE—JOHN 15:5-7

I am the vine; you are the branches. Whoever abides in me and I in him, he it is that bears much fruit, for apart from me you can do nothing. If anyone does not abide in me, he is thrown away like a branch and withers; and the branches are gathered, thrown into the fire, and burned. If you abide in me, and my words abide in you, ask whatever you wish, and it will be done for you.

OPENING PRAYER

Thank you, God, that I do not search my heart alone; you do the searching. Abide with me as I continue to open my heart and all its treasures to you. Give me eyes to see, ears to hear, and a heart to love you more. Amen.

REFLECTION

As we continue to take inventory of our heart's treasures, consider what it means to do all aspects of your life abiding with God. Pause for a moment and tell God that you can do nothing apart from him. Reiterate your intention to do this retreat *with* God.

Now, take about twenty to thirty minutes to do a written inventory of three aspects of your life: your money, your time, and your attention.

Money. Here we will consider our financial treasures. Think through your monthly budget and expenses. Maybe make a pie chart or a laundry list. Where does your money go? Is this where you want it to go? Keep in mind that no one but you needs to see this inventory.

Time. What about your time? Look over the last week and try a block chart to gain an approximate summary of how you spend your days. (If this exercise resonates with you, consider once you get home looking at the screen-time indicator on your smartphone to give you more information. You can also do an hour-by-hour inventory of your week for better clarity.) Do you give God the right of first refusal on your free time?

Overall, do you feel as if, within each day, you have the margin to say yes to what God calls you to? Is your "yes" a "yes" and your "no" a "no"? (see Mt 5:37). If not, why? Where is there space in your calendar to practice holy dawdling with God? By that I mean, picture how much of your time with God is production driven (desiring an outcome) versus time just to *be*, to enjoy him, as with a lover or friend. Why do you think this is?

Attention. Review the section of the introduction on living in an attention economy. What have you given your attention to? Where does your mind wander in prayer? How often do you feel that you engage in self-talk (self-criticism, self-loathing, self-praise) as opposed to God talk: prayer? In silence and solitude are you able to attend to the person of God, or do you feel overwhelmed by your own sense of self (what you want, think, need, or feel)? Do you consider the plans he has for you? (see Jer 29:11). Or is your attention drawn to your own plans?

Remember the call to lose our lives for the sake of the gospel (see Mt 16:25). But we cannot give away what we have yet to claim. We cannot lose our lives (time, money, energy, attention, relationships, or material possessions) if we have not laid hold of our lives and received what God has given us first. Are there places where you find resistance to owning your own life and all its choices and complications? What are they?

Questions for Journaling

- Where do you feel out of control in terms of your time, finances, energy, and attention?
- As you assess these areas, how attached do you feel to these things?
- What are your biggest obstacles to saying yes to God?
- What changes might you need to make?

This was an intense time of introspection. As you close this time, take what lies most heavy on your heart and give it to God; it is not yours to carry. Remember that Jesus alone had perfectly ordered attachments. The rest of us are like octopuses, all our tentacles clinging to the things of this world. God knows this about us; he remembers our frailty, that we are "but dust" (Ps 103:14 NASB). Perhaps the first step to a greater attachment to God might be simply looking at how tethered you are to the things around you that are not him.

Jesus said, "If you abide in me, and my words abide in you, ask whatever you wish, and it will be done for you" (Jn 15:7). What do you want to ask God for right now?

Finish this sentence in your journal, "God, what I most want right now is . . ."

CLOSING PRAYER—PSALM 103:13-14

God, I call to mind that

As a father shows compassion to his children,
so the LORD *shows compassion to those who fear him.*
For he knows our frame;
he remembers that we are dust.

Thank you that you remember how frail I am, and how often I wander away with the wind. God, help me to be similarly compassionate with myself and content with all you have given me. I want to steward my life well with you. Amen.

〉〉〉〉〈〈〈〈

Be gentle with yourself as you go. Consider a slow walk or some time outdoors to sit with your friend Jesus as you look together at all you explored in this time of prayer.

SESSION THREE—AFTERNOON

Abide in My Love

OPENING SCRIPTURE—JOHN 15:9-10

As the Father has loved me, so have I loved you. Abide in my love.
If you keep my commandments, you will abide in my love, just
as I have kept my Father's commandments and abide in his love.

Read this Scripture lectio divina style, reading it several times and pausing between to let God speak in whatever way he wishes. This is not a time for study but a time to be refreshed and nourished by the living Word of God given to you. (Review the lectio divina instructions in chapter two.)

In the second reading, reflect on a word or phrase that shimmered or stood out to you. Give yourself a few minutes to do this. Then ask God, "How does this connect with my life today? What do I need to know or be or do?"

In the third reading, prepare yourself to respond to God.

Questions for Journaling

🖉 Consider how Jesus abides in the Father's love. What does that look like?

🖉 What do you want to ask God about how you understand remaining in his love versus keeping his commandments? Do these feel the same to you? What does God want to say to you about this?

In the fourth reading, simply rest. Do as you are led. Is God asking you to wait on him, hand something over, or rest more deeply in him? Simply rest in the loving presence of God. End this time of prayer by thanking God for calling you to come away and be with him.

Below are questions to guide your reflection on this experience, or if you feel led, simply spend the remaining time of your retreat in silent prayer, keeping your posture of restful contemplation.

REFLECTION

Think about what gives your life energy. What drives you onward? Are you driven from an inner assurance of God's love and purpose for your life or by the demands imposed from outside?

Look broadly over the last few years of your life. In what ways do you see that God has increased your dependence on him by decreasing your dependence on yourself, others, or the systems you have relied on to sustain your life? In other words, How has God allowed disappointment, failure, rejection, loss, and heartache to detach you from the things of this world to form greater dependence on and attachment to him?

How is God asking you to stay close to him, closer maybe than you have been?

What might God be asking you to let go of, so you have room to hold something new? As you consider this question, open your hands as a symbol of opening yourself more deeply to God's love.

>>}}}⊛}}}<<

As you close this time, try to leave the last thirty minutes to an hour of your retreat as a time to remain in this posture of silence as you practice resting in God, who loves you beyond measure.

CLOSING PRAYER

God, I confess the ways in which I have copied the world's idea of a flourishing life: success, money, fame, and comfort. I have aimed to have these things more than I have aimed to have you. Thank you that you are always training your children in dependence. Thank you for the ways you have allowed me to be more dependent on you, more humble, more in need of your grace. This is a gift I receive and do not reject. Help me to do all of life with you. Amen.

>>}}}⊛}}}<<

As you transition into leaving your retreat, leave room to do so slowly, mindfully, and in step with the Spirit. As you pack, consider what you are taking home with you from this retreat.

A BLESSING AS YOU GO

NUMBERS 6:24-26 NKJV

The LORD bless you and keep you;
The LORD make His face shine upon you,
And be gracious to you;
The LORD lift up His countenance upon you,
And give you peace.

Begin by reviewing chapter five, the "Arrival Guide."

....

MORNING—OR UPON ARRIVAL

The Heart's Treasures

OPENING SCRIPTURE—MATTHEW 6:21

Where your treasure is, there your heart will be also.

OPENING PRAYER

God, here I am. I present myself to you and open my heart to you and what you will do on this retreat. Be with me as I assess where my heart and treasures lie, and let me be compassionate with myself, remembering you are always compassionate with me. Amen.

REFLECTION

Jesus was fully attached to his Father, giving him his full focus and attention. Jesus did not have any disordered attachments to anything or anyone. He says of himself, "Truly I say to you, the Son can do nothing of his own accord, but only what he sees the Father doing" (Jn 5:19). His every action was a response to what he saw his Father doing first.

Jesus stresses to his disciples the importance of being rightly attached to him, and therefore his Father as well. "Abide in me, and I in you" (Jn 15:4) was among his final instructions, highlighting the importance of staying attached, connected, and dwelling in him. Yet even the disciples, those who heard Jesus' words at this moment, did not abide perfectly. Thomas Green describes how the disciples' attachment to the things of the world clouded and blocked their ability to be fully open to what God was doing in their midst:

> Their attachments—to honor, to wealth, to security, to life itself—complicated and confused their discernment. . . . They discerned but not infallibly or unerringly. Jesus' discernment was unerring because he was totally open to the Spirit. . . . But most of our lives are like Peter. He loved Jesus; he loved God. . . . [H]e loved "God and" rather than "God only." He truly wanted God's will. But he wanted other things too. And these other wants, which the saints call disordered attachments when they prevent us from floating free in the sea of God, blocked his discernment of Jesus.

In this retreat we will gently take stock of our heart's attachments. Take out paper and a pen as you prepare to open your heart to God. Take a few deep breaths and simply let your mind rest.

Read Matthew 6:19-21, picturing Jesus addressing you personally through these words. As you imagine yourself in this scene, see where your heart wants to go. Spend five to ten minutes in silence dwelling on Jesus' words.

Questions for Journaling

✎ Where does your soul want to go when it doesn't have somewhere else to be, when there are no demands on its time or attention? Be honest here.

✎ When your mind wanders in prayer, what is it showing you?

- ✎ Where do you feel "totally open to the [Holy] Spirit" and what he is doing in your life?
- ✎ Is anything preventing you from "floating free in the sea of God"? What attachments do you carry that might be tethering you to something other than God?
- ✎ Do you see any themes that might connect your heart's treasures? (For example: many of them might revolve around control, the concerns of people pleasing, or about lack of finances).
- ✎ What is sustaining your life right now?
- ✎ How does it feel to attempt to turn your attention to God for the next twenty-four hours?

CLOSING PRAYER

Thank you, God, that your knowledge of me is complete, unerring and unending. Give me the wisdom and clarity I need to explore the landscape of my soul and all the treasures within it. Search me, O God, and know my heart. Test me and know my anxious thoughts. See if there is any offensive, hurtful, or grievous way within me, and lead me in your way everlasting (see Ps 139). Let me see what you want me to see. Protect, seal, and hem in my heart as you promise to do. Amen.

〉〉〉〉❀〈〈〈〈

Close this first session by thanking God for his complete knowledge of and total love for you. Consider meditating on all of Psalm 139 as you take a walk or rest, letting your body lead the way before diving into the afternoon content. As you go, continue to pay attention to what is bubbling up within you, and share it with the Lord as one friend speaks to another.

AFTERNOON

Taking Inventory

OPENING SCRIPTURE—JOHN 15:5-7

I am the vine; you are the branches. Whoever abides in me and I in him, he it is that bears much fruit, for apart from me you can do nothing. If anyone does not abide in me, he is thrown away like a branch and withers; and the branches are gathered, thrown into the fire, and burned. If you abide in me, and my words abide in you, ask whatever you wish, and it will be done for you.

OPENING PRAYER

Thank you, God, that I do not search my heart alone; you do the searching. Abide with me as I continue to open my heart and all its treasures to you. Give me eyes to see, ears to hear, and a heart to love you more. Amen.

REFLECTION

As we continue to take inventory of our heart's treasures, consider what it means to do all aspects of your life abiding with God. Pause for a moment and tell God that you can do nothing apart from him. Reiterate your intention to do this retreat *with* God.

Now, take about twenty to thirty minutes to do a written inventory of three aspects of your life: your money, your time, and your attention.

Money. Here we will consider our financial treasures. Think through your monthly budget and expenses. Maybe make a pie chart or a laundry list. Where does your money go? Is this where you want it to go? Keep in mind that no one but you needs to see this inventory.

Time. What about your time? Look over the last week and try a block chart to gain an approximate summary of how you spend your days. (If this exercise resonates with you, consider once you get home looking at the screen-time indicator on your smartphone to give you more information. You can also do an hour-by-hour inventory of your week for better clarity.) Do you give God the right of first refusal on your free time?

Overall, do you feel as if, within each day, you have the margin to say yes to what God calls you to? Is your "yes" a "yes" and your "no" a "no"? (see Mt 5:37). If not, why? Where is there space in your calendar to practice holy dawdling with God? By that I mean, picture how much of your time with God is production driven (desiring an outcome) versus time just to *be*, to enjoy him, as with a lover or friend. Why do you think this is?

Attention. Review the section of the introduction on living in an attention economy. What have you given your attention to? Where does your mind wander in prayer? How often do you feel that you engage in self-talk (self-criticism, self-loathing, self-praise) as opposed to God talk: prayer? In silence and solitude are you able to attend to the person of God, or do you feel overwhelmed by your own sense of self (what you want, think, need, or feel)? Do you consider the plans he has for you? (see Jer 29:11). Or is your attention drawn to your own plans?

Remember the call to lose our lives for the sake of the gospel (see Mt 16:25). But we cannot give away what we have yet to claim. We cannot lose our lives (time, money, energy, attention, relationships, or material possessions) if we have not laid hold of our lives and received what God has given us first. Are there places where you find resistance to owning your own life and all its choices and complications? What are they?

Questions for Journaling

- Where do you feel out of control in terms of your time, finances, energy, and attention?
- As you assessed these areas, how attached did you feel to these things?
- What are your biggest obstacles to saying yes to God?
- What changes might you need to make?

This was an intense time of introspection. As you close this time, take what lies most heavy on your heart and give it to God; it is not yours to carry. Remember that Jesus alone had perfectly ordered attachments. The rest of us are like octopuses, all our tentacles clinging to the things of this world. God knows this about us; he remembers our frailty, that we are "but dust" (Ps 103:14 NASB). Perhaps the first step to a greater attachment to God might be simply looking at how tethered you are to the things around you that are not him.

Jesus said, "If you abide in me, and my words abide in you, ask whatever you wish, and it will be done for you" (Jn 15:7). What do you want to ask God for right now?

Finish this sentence in your journal, "God, what I most want right now is . . ."

CLOSING PRAYER—PSALM 103:13-14

God, I call to mind that

As a father shows compassion to his children,
  so the LORD shows compassion to those who fear him.
For he knows our frame;
  he remembers that we are dust.

Thank you that you remember how frail I am, and how often I wander away with the wind. God, help me to be similarly compassionate with myself and content with all you have given me. I want to steward my life well with you. Amen.

⁂

Be gentle with yourself as you go. Consider a slow walk or some time outdoors to sit with your friend Jesus as you look together at all you explored in this time of prayer.

EVENING

Abide in My Love

OPENING SCRIPTURE—JOHN 15:9-10

As the Father has loved me, so have I loved you. Abide in my love. If you keep my commandments, you will abide in my love, just as I have kept my Father's commandments and abide in his love.

Read this Scripture lectio divina style, reading it several times and pausing between to let God speak in whatever way he wishes. This is not a time for study but a time to be refreshed and nourished by the living Word of God given to you. (Review the lectio divina instructions in chapter two.)

In the second reading, reflect on a word or phrase that shimmered or stood out to you. Give yourself a few minutes to do this. Then ask God, "How does this connect with my life today? What do I need to know or be or do?"

In the third reading, prepare yourself to respond to God.

Questions for Journaling

🖋 Consider how Jesus abides in the Father's love. What does that look like?

🖋 What do you want to ask God about how you understand remaining in his love versus keeping his commandments? Do these feel the same to you? What does God want to say to you about this?

In the fourth reading, simply rest. Do as you are led. Is God asking you to wait on him, hand something over, or rest more deeply in him? Simply rest in the loving presence of God. End this time of prayer by thanking God for calling you to come away and be with him.

Below are questions to reflect on this experience, or if you feel led, simply spend the remaining time of your retreat in silent prayer, keeping your posture of restful contemplation.

REFLECTION

Think about what gives your life energy; what drives you onward? Are you driven from an inner assurance of God's love and purpose for your life or by the demands imposed from outside?

Look broadly over the last few years of your life. In what ways do you see that God has increased your dependence on him by decreasing your dependence on yourself, others, or the systems you have relied on to sustain your life? In other words, How has God allowed disappointment, failure, rejection, loss, and heartache to detach you from the things of this world to form greater dependence and attachment to him?

How is God asking you to stay close to him, closer maybe than you have been?

What might God be asking you to let go of, so you have room to hold something new?

Close this time with a bow of reverence to God or simply place your hand on your chest, feeling your own heartbeat, as a gesture acknowledging God's care for you and presence with you. Try to leave the last thirty minutes to an hour of your retreat as a time of silence to practice simply resting in God, who loves you beyond measure.

CLOSING PRAYER

God, I confess how I have copied the world's idea of a flourishing life: success, money, fame, and comfort. I have aimed to have these things more than I have aimed to have you. Thank you that you are always training your children in dependence. Thank you for the ways you have allowed me to be more dependent on you, more humble, more in need of your grace. Thank you for showing me all that I cannot do apart from you. This is a gift I receive and do not reject. Help me to do all of life with you. Amen.

>>}}>❖}}}<

Rest, eat a nutritious dinner, and maybe take a slow stroll around your new landscape. Practice being in your own body, if you have been rushed and busy. Practice seeing the scenery, the people, and the natural beauty of your surroundings.

COMPLINE

Read the prayer for compline:

> Keep watch, dear Lord, with those who work, or watch, or weep this night, and give your angels charge over those who sleep. Tend the sick, Lord Christ; give rest to the weary, bless the dying, soothe the suffering, pity the afflicted, shield the joyous; and all for your love's sake. Amen. (Book of Common Prayer 1979)

Spend five minutes looking through your journal, reflecting on all you have experienced today.

End your evening with a prayer of examen:

What was life-giving to you today? Where did you feel the wind at your back?

What was draining for you today? What felt heavy or difficult?

Journal or otherwise explore your responses with God.

Gather together all the parts of yourself and present them to God. Receive this blessing:

> In peace I will lie down and fall asleep, for you alone, O Lord, make me dwell in safety. O come and bless the Lord, all you servants of the Lord, who stand by day and night in the house of the Lord. Lift up your hands to the holy place, and bless the Lord. May the all-powerful Lord grant us a restful night and a peaceful end. Amen.

⟩⟩⟩⟩⟩ DAY TWO ⟨⟨⟨⟨⟨

Rest upon waking. Have coffee in bed or follow any other practice that feels luxurious or comforting as you prepare to rest in Jesus today.

PRAYER OF RECOLLECTION

Move through these three phases of prayer each morning on your retreat, taking as long as you need for each one. Consider incorporating this prayer into your rhythm of life after returning home.

1. *Prayer of presentation.* Dear God, here I am. I present myself to you as one who is holy and pleasing to you. I lay out the pieces of my life before you, and let you see all that is within me. I acknowledge the unilateral nature of your love; all action starts with you. When I come to prayer, I am entering into a conversation I did not start and do not sustain. I wake to a day I did not create, into a universe I do not uphold, into a life I did not earn, and into circumstances I cannot control. Awaken my soul to the reality that I can do nothing apart from you. Thank you, that you are always with me and that I am never alone (see Rom 12:1-2; 8:34; Heb 1:3; Jn 15:5; Mt 28:20).

2. *Prayer of detachment.* Dear God, I let go of anything I try to gain apart from you. I am not defined by my roles: a good or bad mother or father, sister or brother, daughter or son, husband or wife, coworker, student, boss, or friend. These capacities do not define who I am, nor do health or sickness, poverty or wealth, success or

failure, applause or slander. I detach from these roles—however vital and important, they are not at the core of who I am. In places where I have managed to be good, I count Christ more worthy than my success. In areas where I have failed, I ask forgiveness and let go of trying to make something of myself, proving myself to the world, or trying to earn your love, which is given freely (see Phil 3:7-8).

3. *Prayer of attachment.* Dear God, there is nothing you would not do and have not done to make me your own. I receive your mercy and grace. I was created for union with you, and by Jesus' sacrifice, I am saved from separation from you. At my center, I am in you and you are in me. I can only locate my true self in you. I am unrighteous on my own, but you are my righteousness. I am chaotic on my own, but you have given me the rightly ordered mind of Christ. Because you have attached me to yourself and will never let me go, I have full forgiveness, freedom, acceptance, and pardon from my sin, guilt, and shame. I am blameless in your sight. You delight in me and delight to co-labor with me in the unique, good work you have called me to. I am precious and irreplaceable to you. No matter the circumstance in which I find myself, I know that nothing comes to me that did not first pass through the cross. No matter what else is true of me in this life, at the center of my being is beloved belonging; I am a child of God. There is nowhere I can run where you will not follow, nowhere I can hide where you will not find me.

No matter how deep I go into my soul with you, I will find love, all the way down (see Col 1:22; Gal 2:20; Col 2:13-15; Rom 8:16; Ps 139:7-12).

Questions for Journaling

✎ Which of these, if any, is difficult for your soul to receive?
✎ Where are you feeling open to God today?
✎ Which of these, if any, is hard for you to detach from?
✎ What truths were you able to receive fully? Confess any unbelief.

MORNING

A Better View

OPENING SCRIPTURE—LUKE 5:3 NIV

[Jesus] got into one of the boats, the one belonging to Simon, and asked him to put out a little from the shore. Then he sat down and taught the people from the boat.

OPENING PRAYER

Jesus, you were never harried nor frantic. Faced with endless demands, repetitive needs, and the tugging and pulling of the crowd, still you walked gently on the earth. Let me walk gently into today. Let me keep pace with you. Give me courage and let me learn from you. Amen.

REFLECTION

Take a few deep breaths, and for the next five to ten minutes, imagine you are in this boat. Imagine the breeze, or the waves rocking the boat slightly. Imagine the sights, sounds, and smells. Try to imagine you are in this privileged place next to Jesus. How does it feel? How do you want to respond?

Pushed away from the shore, he has a better vantage point to see the crowds with all their varied desires and needs. This kind of space offers clarity. Consider this new point of view now that you have been away from home, your normal schedule, and the demands of others for twenty-four hours.

Questions for Journaling

- ✐ What can you now see on the shore of your life that you could not at the beginning of your retreat?
- ✐ Return to this question from yesterday: What is sustaining your life right now? Has anything changed for you in the last twenty-four hours?
- ✐ What did you bring into this retreat with you?
- ✐ What are you leaving behind? Release all of these to the Lord and affirm who you are in him—beloved, free, delightful, celebrated child, and heir.
- ✐ How have you been able to turn your attention to God?
- ✐ What has that been like for you?
- ✐ What will you carry with you out of this retreat?

Try to spend the last thirty minutes to an hour of your retreat in silence. End by entrusting yourself to God, who knows you, cares for you, delights in time spent with you, and loves you completely.

As you transition into leaving your retreat, even as you pack up your belongings, leave room to do it slowly, mindfully, and in step with the Spirit.

A BLESSING AS YOU GO

NUMBERS 6:24-26 NKJV

The LORD bless you and keep you;
The LORD make His face shine upon you,
And be gracious to you;
The LORD lift up His countenance upon you,
And give you peace.

⇢⇢⇥⇥ DAY ONE ⇤⇤⇠⇠

Begin by reviewing chapter five, the "Arrival Guide."

....

AFTERNOON

Abiding

OPENING SCRIPTURE—JOHN 15:4

Abide in me, and I in you. As the branch cannot bear fruit by itself, unless it abides in the vine, neither can you, unless you abide in me.

OPENING PRAYER

God, I choose to come away with you for this time. I let go of any concerns or distractions that might keep me from attaching myself to you, your heart, your interests, your love. Help me wade out into deeper waters with you. Teach me what it means to be sustained by your love. Amen.

REFLECTION

In biblical Greek, *menō* translates to "abide." It also means: sustain, continue, dwell, endure, be present, remain, stand, and tarry. Of these verbs, which one stands out the most to you right now? Why?

Sit with God in prayer for a few moments, settling into your breath, and ask God what it means for you to abide in him during this time.

Psalm 42 offers many illustrations of the shape a soul might take. The psalmist describes a soul in despair and "cast

down," and like a tornado "in turmoil within me" (Ps 42:5).
There is also a soul that "thirsts" for God, parched and dehydrated (Ps 42:2). In the above Scripture, Jesus refers to the
soul as deeply dependent, unable to sustain life on its own.

Take a moment and visualize your soul's condition. When
you are ready, draw a picture, or use clay or Play-Doh if you
brought it, to represent the shape or state of your soul right now.

Questions for Journaling

> ✐ What state is your soul in; what shape might it take?
> ✐ What is sustaining your life right now?
> ✐ Where are you longing to tarry (or practice holy daw-
>   dling) with God?
> ✐ How does it feel to attempt to turn your attention to God
>   for the next forty-eight hours?

CLOSING PRAYER

God, only you know the depths of my heart. Draw out what
I most need to see on this retreat (see Prov 20:5). Help me
to give you my full attention. Help me to rest in the steady
gaze of your love. I leave behind my tasks and lists, my obligations and demands. I give them into your capable hands.
Let my heart will your way and rest in your love. Amen.

⋙⋙✦⋘⋘

Spend more time familiarizing yourself with your new surroundings, taking a walk before or after dinner.

EVENING

Attachments

OPENING SCRIPTURE—JOHN 15:9

As the Father has loved me, so have I loved you. Abide in my love.

OPENING PRAYER

Take five minutes to sit quietly and breathe deeply. Meditate on this passage, reading it several times. Allow your attention to rest completely on the love God has for Jesus; the love God has for you.

REFLECTION

Jesus was fully attached to his Father, giving him his full focus and attention. Jesus did not have any disordered attachments to anything or anyone. He says of himself, "Truly I say to you, the Son can do nothing of his own accord, but only what he sees the Father doing" (Jn 5:19). His every action was a response to what he saw his Father doing first.

Jesus stresses to his disciples the importance of being rightly attached to him, and therefore his Father as well. "Abide in me, and I in you" (Jn 15:4) was among his final instructions, highlighting the importance of staying attached, connected, and dwelling in him. Yet even the disciples, those who heard Jesus' words at this moment, did not abide perfectly. Thomas Green describes how the disciples' attachment to the things of the world clouded and blocked their ability to be fully open to what God was doing in their midst:

Their attachments—to honor, to wealth, to security, to life itself—complicated and confused their discernment ... They discerned but not infallibly or unerringly. Jesus' discernment was unerring because he was totally open to the Spirit ... But most of our lives are like Peter. He loved Jesus; he loved God. ... [H]e loved "God and" rather than "God only." He truly wanted God's will. But he wanted other things too. And these other wants, which the saints call disordered attachments when they prevent us from floating free in the sea of God, blocked his discernment of Jesus.

God gently invites us to detach from the things we can see, know, and rely on to help us move into places of interior freedom. When we are overly attached to finite realities, we are not free to say yes to what he invites us into. As you engage with the journaling prompts, consider places within yourself where you do or do not feel free to say yes to what God is calling you to.

Questions for Journaling

- In what ways do you see that God has increased your dependence on him by decreasing your dependence on yourself, others, or the systems you have relied on to sustain your life? In other words, How has God allowed disappointment, failure, rejection, loss, and heartache to detach you from the things of this world to form greater dependence and attachment to him?
- Where does your soul want to go when it doesn't have somewhere else to be, when there are no demands on its time or attention? What does it gravitate toward? Be honest here.

> ✐ Where do you feel "totally open to the [Holy] Spirit" and what he is doing in your life?
> ✐ What is preventing you from "floating free in the sea of God"? What attachments do you carry that might be tethering you to something other than God?

CLOSING PRAYER

Thank you, God, that you keep me close to you. It is your easy yoke that ties me to you, helping me travel where you lead. Thank you that neither death nor life, neither angels nor demons, neither my fears for today nor my worries about tomorrow—not even the powers of hell—can separate me from your great love (see Rom 8:38-39). Amen.

〉〉〉〉〉🕸〈〈〈〈〈

Close this evening session by thanking God for his complete knowledge of and total love for you. As you go, continue to pay attention to what you feel attached to and share it with the Lord as one friend speaks to another.

COMPLINE

Read the prayer for compline.

> Keep watch, dear Lord, with those who work, or watch, or weep this night, and give your angels charge over those who sleep. Tend the sick, Lord Christ; give rest to the weary, bless the dying, soothe the suffering, pity the afflicted, shield the joyous; and all for your love's sake. Amen. (Book of Common Prayer 1979)

Spend five minutes looking through your journal, reflecting on all you have experienced today.

End your evening with a prayer of examen:

What was life-giving to you today? Where did you feel the wind at your back?

What was draining for you today? What felt heavy or difficult?

Journal or otherwise explore these with God.

⋊⋊⋊⋈⋊⋊⋊⋉

Gather together all the parts of yourself and present them to God. Receive this blessing:

> In peace I will lie down and fall asleep, for you alone, O Lord, make me dwell in safety. O come and bless the Lord, all you servants of the Lord, who stand by day and night in the house of the Lord. Lift up your hands to the holy place, and bless the Lord. May the all-powerful Lord grant us a restful night and a peaceful end. Amen.

⋊⋊⋈ DAY TWO ⋈⋉⋉

Rest upon waking. Have coffee in bed or follow any other practice that feels luxurious or comforting as you prepare to rest in Jesus today.

PRAYER OF RECOLLECTION

Move through these three phases of prayer each morning on your retreat, taking as long as you need on each one. Consider incorporating this prayer into your rhythm of life after returning home.

1. *Prayer of presentation.* Dear God, here I am. I present myself to you as one who is holy and pleasing to you. I lay out the pieces of my life before you and let you see all that is within me. I acknowledge the unilateral nature of your love; all action starts with you. When I come to prayer, I am entering into a conversation I did not start and do not sustain. I wake to a day I did not create, a universe I do not uphold, a life I did not earn, and circumstances I cannot control. Awaken my soul to the reality that I can do nothing apart from you. Thank you that you are always with me and that I am never alone (see Rom 12:1-2; 8:34; Heb 1:3; Jn 15:5; Mt 28:20).

2. *Prayer of detachment.* Dear God, I let go of anything I try to gain apart from you. I am not defined by my roles: a good or bad mother or father, sister or brother, daughter or son, husband or wife, coworker, student, boss, or friend. These capacities do not define who I am, nor does health or sickness, poverty or wealth, success or failure, applause or slander. I detach from these roles—however vital and important, they are not at the core of who I am. In places where I have managed to be good, I count Christ more worthy than my success. In areas where I have failed, I ask for-giveness and let go of trying to make something of myself, proving myself to the world, or trying to earn your love, which is given freely (see Phil 3:7-8).

3. *Prayer of attachment.* Dear God, there is nothing you would not do and have not done to make me your

own. I receive your mercy and grace. I was created for union with you, and by Jesus' sacrifice, I am saved from separation from you. At my center, I am in you and you are in me. I can only locate my true self in you. I am unrighteous on my own, but you are my righteousness. I am chaotic on my own, but you have given me the rightly ordered mind of Christ. Because you have attached me to yourself and will never let me go, I have full forgiveness, freedom, acceptance, and pardon from my sin, guilt, and shame. I am blameless in your sight. You delight in me, and delight to co-labor with me in the good work you have uniquely called me to. I am precious and irreplaceable to you. No matter the circumstance in which I find myself, I know that nothing comes to me that did not first pass through the cross. No matter what else is true of me in this life, at the center of my being is beloved belonging; I am a child of God. There is nowhere I can run where you will not follow, nowhere I can hide where you will not find me. No matter how deep I go into my soul with you, I will find love, all the way down (see Col 1:22; Gal 2:20; Col 2:13-15; Rom 8:16; Ps 139:7-12).

Questions for Journaling

🖉 Which of these, if any, is difficult for your soul to receive?

🖉 Where are you feeling open to God today?

🖉 Which of these, if any, is hard for you to detach from?

🖉 What truths were you able to receive fully? Confess any unbelief.

MORNING

Better Springs

OPENING SCRIPTURE—MATTHEW 6:21

Where your treasure is, there your heart will be also.

OPENING PRAYER

Thank you, God, that your knowledge of me is complete, unerring, and unending. Give me the wisdom and clarity I need to explore the landscape of my soul and all the treasure within it. Search me, O God, and know my heart. Test me and know my anxious thoughts. See if there is any offensive, hurtful, or grievous way within me, and lead me in your way everlasting (see Ps 139). Let me see what you want me to see, and protect, seal, and hem in my heart as you promise to do. Amen.

REFLECTION

Today we will take an inventory of the heart and its treasures. In our morning session we will cover exercises one and two, and in the afternoon session, exercise three. Our evening session will tie together all we have explored today.

Take out paper and a pen as you prepare to open your heart to God. Take a few deep breaths and simply let your mind rest.

EXERCISE ONE

To the woman at the well, Jesus described our life with God as a spring of water that "bubbles up into eternal life." (Jn 4:14 CEB)

Read Matthew 6:19-21, picturing Jesus addressing you personally through these words. As you imagine yourself in this scene, see where your heart wants to go. Do your best not to make judgments. You are honestly assessing what your heart treasures. This is good and useful information. See where your soul settles. What does your soul land on? Take note of what feels important to you, what you're concerned about, and where your mind wanders.

Spend five to ten minutes in silence dwelling on Jesus' words.

Questions for Journaling

- ✐ What is bubbling up; rising to the surface?
- ✐ Where does your soul want to go when it doesn't have somewhere else to be, when there are no demands on its time or attention? Be honest here.
- ✐ What does it want to tell you? What is it showing you?

EXERCISE TWO

For the next ten to fifteen minutes, consider Genesis 16:7-8 where we find Hagar alone in the desert with God. She is not there by choice but was forced into the wilderness at the hands of her abusive master.

"The angel of the LORD found her by a spring of water in the wilderness, the spring on the way to Shur. And he said, 'Hagar, servant of Sarai, where have you come from and where are you going?'"

God addresses Hagar against the backdrop of a spring bubbling up in the wilderness. He asks a powerful question appropriate for retreat time: "Where have you come from and where are you going?"

The Spirit of God addresses Hagar by a spring of water. She is presumably there because any refreshment she had brought with her had run dry. Consider this setting in terms of your own internal landscape.

Turn your attention toward God, letting him address you directly with this question: *Where has your soul been and where is it going?* Ask God to reveal what he wants you to see. In case you feel stuck here, there are some common threads that often come up in spiritual inventories: worry, fear, and shame are a few. Do you find yourself fixated on a certain conversation and interaction? Explore why that is with God; ask for wisdom and clarity. Do you feel shame blanketing your soul? Ask God to tease out different emotions, especially as you explore anger and fear. Tell God directly what is coming up for you.

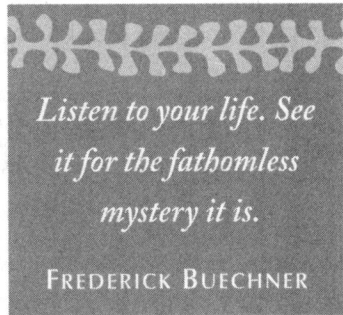

> *Listen to your life. See it for the fathomless mystery it is.*
>
> FREDERICK BUECHNER

Questions for Journaling

- What is your life itself telling you? What does your life say you treasure?
- Where has your soul been? What has it loved? Where is it wanting to go?
- Where have you run dry? Where is God offering you a better spring?

CLOSING PRAYER

Thank you, God, that you have put a spring of living water within me that will never run dry and wells up to eternal life. Remind me of this truth that I so often forget: that you alone refresh my soul. Amen.

....

AFTERNOON

The Heart's Treasures

OPENING SCRIPTURE—JOHN 15:5-7

I am the vine; you are the branches. Whoever abides in me and I in him, he it is that bears much fruit, for apart from me you can do nothing. If anyone does not abide in me, he is thrown away like a branch and withers; and the branches are gathered, thrown into the fire and burned. If you abide in me, and my words abide in you, ask whatever you wish, and it will be done for you.

OPENING PRAYER

God, as I continue to look at the state of my soul, I am aware that I do not want to do this alone. I can do nothing apart from you. I want to do this and all of life with you. Be merciful to me in this time. Give me eyes to see, ears to hear, and a heart to love you more. Amen.

EXERCISE THREE

Now, take about twenty to thirty minutes to do a written inventory of three aspects of your life: your money, your time, and your attention.

Money. Here we will consider our financial treasures. Think through your monthly budget and expenses. Maybe make a pie chart or a laundry list. Where does your money go? Is this where you want it to go? Keep in mind that no one but you needs to see this inventory.

Time. What about your time? Look over the last week and try a block chart to gain an approximate summary of how you spend your days. (If this exercise resonates with you, consider once you get home looking at the screen-time indicator on your smartphone to give you more information. You can also do an hour-by-hour inventory of your week for better clarity.) Do you give God the right of first refusal on your free time?

Overall, do you feel as if, within each day, you have the margin to say yes to what God calls you to? Is your "yes" a "yes" and your "no" a "no"? (see Mt 5:37). If not, why? Where is there space in your calendar to practice holy dawdling with God? By that I mean, picture how much of your time with God is production driven (desiring an outcome) versus time just to *be*, to enjoy him, as with a lover or friend. Why do you think this is?

Attention. Review the section of the introduction on living in an attention economy. What have you given your attention to? Where does your mind wander in prayer? How often do you feel that you engage in self-talk (self-criticism, self-loathing, self-praise) as opposed to God talk: prayer? In silence and solitude are you able to attend to the person of God, or do you feel overwhelmed by your own sense of self (what you want, think, need, or feel)? Do you consider the plans he has for you? (see Jer 29:11). Or is your attention drawn to your own plans?

Remember the call to lose our lives for the sake of the gospel (see Mt 16:25). But we cannot give away what we have yet to claim. We cannot lose our lives (time, money, energy, attention, relationships, or material possessions) if we have not laid hold of our lives and received what God has given us first. Are there places where you find resistance to owning your own life and all its choices and complications? What are they?

Questions for Journaling

- ✎ Where do you feel out of control in terms of your time, finances, energy, and attention?
- ✎ As you assessed these areas, how attached did you feel to these things?
- ✎ What are your biggest obstacles to saying yes to God?
- ✎ What changes might you need to make?

REFLECTION

Today's exercises and Scriptures have opened us up to the frailty of the human condition. We are utterly incapable of doing a single thing on our own (see Jn 15:5). With God, we are robustly fruitful children, bubbling up with new life. Quite a contrast.

Jesus said, "If you abide in me, and my words abide in you, ask whatever you wish, and it will be done for you" (Jn 15:7). What do you want to ask God for right now?

Finish this sentence in your journal, "God, what I most want right now is . . ."

Today held an intense time of introspection. As you close this time, take what lies most heavy on your heart and give it to God; it is not yours to carry. Remember that Jesus alone had perfectly ordered attachments. The rest of us are like octopuses, all our tentacles clinging to the things of this world. God knows this about us; he remembers our frailty, that we are "but dust" (Ps 103:14 NASB). Perhaps the first step to a greater attachment to God might be simply looking at how tethered you are to the things around you that are not him.

Be gentle with yourself as you go. Consider a slow walk or some time outdoors to sit with your friend Jesus as you look together at all you explored in this time of prayer.

CLOSING PRAYER

God, I thank you for showing me places in my life where I am "God and" instead of "God only." Help me as I look at all that I am attached to that is not of you. Thank you for being compassionate with me; you know my frame; you remember that I am dust (see Ps 103:13-14). I am also deeply valuable to you and precious in your sight (see Is 43:4) and can never be thrown away. Amen.

EVENING

Abide in My Love

OPENING SCRIPTURE—JOHN 15:9-10

As the Father has loved me, so have I loved you. Abide in my love. If you keep my commandments, you will abide in my love, just as I have kept my Father's commandments and abide in his love.

Read this Scripture lectio divina style, reading it several times and pausing between to let God speak in whatever way he wishes. This is not a time for study but a time to be refreshed and nourished by the living Word of God given to you. (Review the four movements of lectio divina in chapter two.)

In the second reading, reflect on a word or phrase that shimmered or stood out to you. Give yourself a few minutes to do this. Then ask God, "How does this connect with my life today? What do I need to know or be or do?"

In the third reading, prepare yourself to respond to God.

Questions for Journaling

- Consider how Jesus abides in the Father's love. What does that look like? Maybe ask him questions about it or listen to what he wants to say about that to you right now.
- What do you want to say to God about how you understand remaining in his love versus keeping his commandments? Which of these feels more challenging for you to do (love or obey)?
- Compared to a year ago, where do you see that God has increased your dependence on him by decreasing your dependence on yourself, others, or the systems you have relied on to sustain your life? In other words, How has God allowed disappointment, failure, rejection, loss, and heartache to detach you from the things of this world to form greater dependence and attachment to him? How does it feel to value your life by these metrics?

In the fourth reading, simply rest. Do as you are led. Is God asking you to wait on him, hand something over, or rest more deeply in him? Simply rest in the loving presence of

God. End this time of prayer by thanking God for calling you to come away and be with him where he is.

Below are prompts to reflect on this experience, or if you feel led, simply spend the remaining time of this session in silent prayer, keeping your posture of restful contemplation.

REFLECTION

To deepen your experience of lectio divina, pay attention to which words of this Scripture shimmered or stood out to you. Write those words down with either a colored pencil or marker, and as you meditate on them, doodle around each word separately or as a whole.

"Holy Scripture cries aloud!" But are we listening? Have we ordered our lives so there is space and time to listen and to respond? The "word 'obedience' is derived from the Latin *oboedire*, which shares its roots with *audire*, to hear. So to obey really means to hear and then act on what we have heard, or, in other words, to see that the listening achieves its aim. We are not being truly attentive unless we are prepared to act on what we hear."

How is God asking you to stay close to him, closer maybe than you have been?

What might God be asking you to let go of, so you have room to hold something new?

What would it mean to actively obey the command to abide more deeply in your life?

What stands out to you about what you drew around the Scripture?

CLOSING PRAYER

God, I confess how I have copied the world's idea of a flourishing life: success, money, fame, and comfort. I have aimed to have these things more than I have aimed to have you. Thank you that you are always training your children in dependence. Thank you for the ways you have allowed me to be more dependent on you, more humble, more in need of your grace. This is a gift I receive and do not reject. Help me to do all of life with you. Amen.

〉〉〉〉〈❀〉〉〉〉〈

Close your time of prayer with a bow of reverence to God or simply place your hand to your chest, feeling your own heartbeat, as a gesture acknowledging God's care for you and presence with you.

Rest, eat a nutritious dinner, and maybe take a slow stroll around your new landscape. Practice being in your own body, if you have been rushed and busy. Practice seeing the scenery, the people, and the natural beauty of your surroundings.

COMPLINE

Read the prayer for compline.

Keep watch, dear Lord, with those who work, or watch, or weep this night, and give your angels charge over those who sleep. Tend the sick, Lord Christ; give rest to the weary, bless the dying, soothe the suffering, pity the afflicted, shield the joyous; and all for your love's sake. Amen. (Book of Common Prayer 1979)

Spend five minutes looking through your journal, reflecting on all you have experienced today.

End your evening with a prayer of examen:

What was life-giving to you today? Where did you feel the wind at your back?

What was draining for you today? What felt heavy or difficult?

Journal or otherwise explore these with God.

}}}}{❀}}}}{

Today we saw that there are parts of our hearts that are "God and" and parts of our hearts that are "God only." God knows the nature of our fickle, fractured hearts and loves us with a love that unites those pieces. He alone holds everything together (see Col 1:17).

Gather together all the parts of yourself and present them to God. Receive this blessing:

> In peace I will lie down and fall asleep, for you alone, O Lord, make me dwell in safety. O come and bless the Lord, all you servants of the Lord, who stand by day and night in the house of the Lord. Lift up your hands to the holy place, and bless the Lord. May the all-powerful Lord grant us a restful night and a peaceful end. Amen.

}}}}{ DAY THREE }{{{{

Rest upon waking. Have coffee in bed or follow any other practice that feels luxurious or comforting as you prepare to rest in Jesus today.

PRAYER OF RECOLLECTION

Refer to day two.

....

MORNING

A Better View

OPENING SCRIPTURE—LUKE 5:3 NIV

[Jesus] got into one of the boats, the one belonging to Simon, and asked him to put out a little from shore. Then he sat down and taught the people from the boat.

OPENING PRAYER

Jesus, you were never harried nor frantic. Faced with endless demands, repetitive needs, and the tugging and pulling of the crowd, still you walked gently on the earth. Let me walk gently into today. Let me keep pace with you. Give me courage and let me learn from you. Amen.

REFLECTION

Take a few deep breaths, and for the next five to ten minutes, imagine you are in this boat. Imagine the breeze or the waves rocking the boat slightly. Imagine the sights, sounds, and smells. Try to imagine you are in this privileged place next to Jesus. How does it feel? How do you want to respond?

Pushed away from the shore, he has a better vantage point to see the crowds with all their varied desires and needs. This kind of space offers clarity. Consider this new point of view now that you have been away from home, your normal schedule, and the demands of others for over twenty-four hours.

Questions for Journaling

🖋 What can you now see on the shore of your life that you could not at the beginning of your retreat?

> ✐ Return to this question from yesterday: What is sustaining your life right now? Has anything changed for you in the last twenty-four hours? If so, what?
>
> ✐ What did you bring into this retreat with you?
>
> ✐ What are you leaving behind? Release all of these to the Lord and affirm who you are in him—beloved, free, delightful, celebrated child, and heir.
>
> ✐ How have you been able to turn your attention to God?
>
> ✐ What has that been like for you?
>
> ✐ What will you carry with you out of this retreat?

Try to spend the last thirty minutes to an hour of your retreat in silence. End by entrusting yourself to God, who knows you, cares for you, delights in time spent with you, and loves you completely.

As you transition into leaving your retreat, even as you pack up your belongings, leave room to do it slowly, mindfully, and in step with the Spirit.

A BLESSING AS YOU GO

NUMBERS 6:24-26 NKJV

The LORD bless you and keep you;
The LORD make His face shine upon you,
And be gracious to you;
The LORD lift up His countenance upon you,
And give you peace.

FOR ONE WHO IS WEARY

✝

Only on the rarest of occasions does God give us work we can finish. Most of our daily labor—from the filing of taxes to the planting of gardens—requires repetitive, perpetual work. Year in and year out, season by season, we do work that can never be completed. We participate in the cycle of life, bringing people into the world and walking them out of it. From Scripture's opening in Genesis to its close in Revelation, we find a God who invites us into a healthy rhythm of work and rest, and we see the people of God constantly struggle in the balance.

Years ago, my husband built me a vegetable garden: raised wood beds on a rectangle of pea gravel. We designed it, irrigated it, and planted all my favorite things in one place. My little garden restores my soul in a way that is hard to explain. Learning to move with the seasons, tend to the soil, eradicate weeds, and vigilantly water—all these elements have trained my soul toward God and the ways of his kingdom. This plot of land remains one of the few places where the repetition of work has not lost its luster.

The harvest from this little garden has reduced bit by bit over the years. I made the mistake of planting an herb section including mint. Several people reading this just clutched their pearls. Mint invades every inch it can. It became so invasive that I spent months hunting down suckers. No matter how often I dug, I found wiry clumps of roots everywhere, choking out anything I planted.

After excavating all I could, my plants still withered, each harvest producing less than the year before. I changed my seed supplier; I watched vigilantly for bugs, mold, and the gophers who love to pop in for a head of lettuce. But no matter how much I learned or how often I amended my soil, nothing was working.

Last winter, I found clumps of roots, which I assumed were more mint, until I stopped plucking it at the surface and went down to the base. I spent an hour vigorously shoving soil aside as the root went deeper and widened significantly. Finally, I was left looking at the base of my garden; a mesh layer my husband had laid to deter gophers was cracked, warped, and upended by enormous roots. The more I investigated, the more I found these roots snaking everywhere, tying everything up. They were not mint suckers, they were tree roots: old, established magnolia, sycamore, and fig that I had planted the garden beneath. I have since learned that you never place a vegetable garden near mature trees, especially ones with robust root systems.

I spent weeks, maybe months, uprooting every last runner I could find, knowing full well that my efforts were in vain. These roots will keep growing, and I will keep digging until I change the location of my garden. However, it has made all the difference knowing what I am dealing with. I open this retreat on weariness with this image of seeing the roots in our lives because we must first reckon with what is choking out the life within before we can hope to dig it out. This knowledge alone may prove helpful enough to remove what is depleting. However, it might illuminate realities you cannot immediately change but must live with, at least for now. There are phases of life where we must learn to endure a thorn in the flesh or a root in the garden. God's grace is enough there too.

Weariness can take on many forms, and naming with accuracy the reality of your soul's exhaustion helps find its rest. The end is the same—rest in the presence of God—but we must first name a few things to get there. I've named four types of weariness that will inform our retreat rhythm. This is by no means an exhaustive list but rather enough to get your soul engaged to wonder with God on the root cause of your weariness.

FOUR TYPES OF SOUL WEARINESS

Weariness of sin. We live in a world pervaded by sin: sin from within ourselves, in those we meet, and in systems of corruption and abuse all over the globe. We cannot escape the reality that we are born into a sinful and broken world. Sin affects us daily, but certain in-breaking moments make us more aware of it.

Corporately, we've become afraid of the word *sin* and have done quite a bit of work to distance ourselves from it. We may sin consistently, feel its effects from others, swim in its waters all around us, yet call it names like *brokenness* or *messiness.* Changing the language does nothing to alter our condition. In fact, I think it does a great disservice to the state of our souls to refuse to name it properly. It leaves us burdened and without a solution to our ailments when Jesus has already provided a solution to our sin problem.

In the Protestant church I attend, we are not often given space to unburden ourselves from the sin that weighs us down. I've been in church communities before where this has been part of the rhythm of the liturgy, so I feel its loss. Corporate confession is valuable, but so is personal confession. I see many people who come in for spiritual direction looking for a place to unburden themselves. They need someone to bear witness as they give an honest account. In one way or another, they say: *This is the reality of my soul, I need to come out of hiding, I'm done pretending.* It is not my role to formally absolve sin, but we both find the words lose their power somewhere between their lips to my ears. I have seen souls leave my office lighter. We must recapture the gift of confession, both corporate and private, as God's gift to unburden us. We cannot carry sin forever, and if it is allowed to pile up in our souls, over time, it wears us down.

Weariness of pain. On the other hand, not all that wears us down is sin. Some of us become compulsive about confessing sin as though every phobia and obsession we've developed over a lifetime sprang up from the earth unbidden. We are birthed into families and systems that are broken, that knowingly and unknowingly cause us pain. We are fully formed, neurotic beings before we ever consider our spiritual formation. Hebrews 12:1-2 says, "Let us also lay aside every weight, and sin which clings so closely, and let us run with endurance the race that is set before us, looking to Jesus, the founder and perfecter of our faith." Here the author of Hebrews parcels out things that hold us back, weigh us down, and cause our weariness. The author says to lay aside both weight *and* sin, offering two distinct categories to understand what saps our endurance. There is sin (our own or others') that holds us back. There is also weight that holds us back and hinders our advancement. What does that weight consist of? Depression, panic, fear? What in our lives slows us down, dampens our faith, or hinders our growth in addition to sin? What are we carrying around that is heavy, perhaps because we were never meant to carry it?

At least in part, we might conceptualize this weight as pain. We carry around every lived experience in our bodies. There are pain points in our lives that can look like coping strategies, survival skills, or things that perhaps helped us endure in dysfunctional homes growing up, giving us a needed respite in traumatic circumstances. There is also embodied trauma, compounded over years, that manifests as a myriad of ailments.

There is chronic pain and illness along with the malaise that descends after years of misdiagnoses from an often-dismissive medical field. There are the unwanted house-guests of depression and anxiety and the awareness that even if they can be managed, they often never leave. There are self-sabotaging behaviors, critical inner monologues, and people-pleasing tendencies. There are codependent behaviors we have relied on, spending a lifetime doing for others what they can do for themselves while wondering why we are so tired all the time.

When we address sin, it's called repentance; when we address pain, it's called healing.

Weariness from doing good. There is a weariness that comes from living between two kingdoms. We exist in the world with all its shiny promises, cultural demands, and responsibilities. The currency here is success, wealth, self-promotion, and hustle. But we belong to another kingdom that Jesus brought with him, and it is this kingdom's values we aim to live by. In walking with Jesus, we confront the reality of these opposing kingdoms and the difficult call on our lives to live in both. We are in the world but not of it (see Jn 17:16). We are to keep our eyes set on Jesus' return, to wait and watch as he taught in so many of his parables (see Mt 24:42). Yet we are also called to engage in acts of justice and service. We are to love our neighbors in their brokenness in pain (see Mk 12:31). We are to seek to serve and be last in a world that says being first is far better (see Mk 9:35). Plus we have to pay our bills and stock the fridge. We are not monastics off in their caves devoted to praying the hours. We must keep the lights on. In many ways, this makes us a type of exile (see Heb 11:13). We are under a ruling authority opposed to God as we make our way through the earth as citizens of heaven (see Phil 3:20).

This means we are constantly enticed to take shortcuts, cut side deals, cheat, lie—essentially do things the world's way. The apostle Paul says, "Do not be deceived: God is not mocked, for whatever one sows, that will he also reap. For the one who sows to his own flesh will from the flesh reap corruption, but the one who sows to the Spirit will from the Spirit reap eternal life. And let us not grow weary of doing good, for in due season we will reap, if we do not give up" (Gal 6:7-9). Paul suggests a bone-deep weariness for believers sowing spiritual seed in a world of soil-packed corruption. We do not see the fruit of our labors. It turns out that for the time being, often the last *are* last and the choice to serve is thankless and exhausting. The kids grow up and move out and make their own baffling choices, and those we minister to at home or work seem immovable and unchanged. The landscape of our efforts looks meager at best, and we are tempted to throw in the towel.

Weariness from spiritual bypassing. This type of weariness often gets overlooked. In our day-to-day lives, there is much grief, pain, sin, and darkness we must address to have an integrated soul. We can only pretend "Everything is fine!" for so long until we cannot. When we fail to attend to the reality of our inner lives, we ignore, numb, or distract ourselves instead. In her book *Healing Through the Dark Emotions*, Miriam Greenspan explains how we exhaust ourselves trying not to feel what we might deem dark or negative emotions. She says, "Dark emotions don't go away. They simply come to us in whatever form we can bear."

In the church especially, we might be tempted to think any problem can be solved with enough faith. This spiritual bypassing, often a defense mechanism, inevitably hinders our faith instead of growing it. Often spiritual bypassing glosses over the issue, claiming forgiveness, peace, or faith over situations and people that require curiosity, repentance, and presence. It is why it is so painful when pat answers or pithy Bible quotes are given in response to deep pain and loss, like quoting Romans 8:28 (CEB), that "God works all things together for good" at a child's funeral.

Spiritual bypassing creates long-term damage to our souls and psyches when we refuse to engage with our negative emotions. Denying them, forcing them away, numbing, and distracting ourselves from them expends far more energy than it would take to listen to, attend, and learn from them. The earliest Christians understood that God was active in our dark emotions, and the experience of God's absence was in no way an indication of the reality of his presence. The temptation is to try to make our way *around* the darkness when God beckons us to come *near* it with him (see Ex 20:21). We do well to remember that the good shepherd's rod and staff comfort us in the dark valley, because they signify his authority over and presence in life's darkest places (see Ps 23:4).

For some, these four movements explored in the next three days will move you through your weariness in increasing depth. For others, however, the root cause of weariness will be so apparent that you will need to pay extra attention to those parts of the retreat. Be sure to allow God to guide your time, not what I have written here. If you come into this retreat well aware that a pain point in your life is bleeding you of energy and life, feel free to stay with those images and verses for the entirety of your time. I have purposely included an abundance of content within each section, so if you feel the call to linger there at the expense of other places, you are free to do so. It is Jesus, who "daily bears us up" (Ps 68:19)—with whom you are yoked—who is leading this time. Go where he wants to take you.

〉〉〉〉⧉〈〈〈〈

Begin by reviewing chapter five, the "Arrival Guide."

....

AFTERNOON

The Easy Yoke

OPENING SCRIPTURE—MATTHEW 11:28-30 NIV

Come to me, all you who are weary and burdened, and I will give you rest. Take my yoke upon you and learn from me, for I am gentle and humble in heart, and you will find rest for your souls. For my yoke is easy and my burden is light.

OPENING PRAYER

Lord, I acknowledge my lack, my exhaustion, my deep weariness. I cannot be all things to all people; I can't do all the things required of me; and I feel this reality deep in my bones. I cannot_____. (Talk to God here about all that comes to mind.) I surrender everything to you, laying down all that I carry: every person, every problem, every responsibility, every deadline. I entrust all I have into your capable hands. Amen.

REFLECTION

Take a few moments to sit in silence with God, asking him to give you a sense of what is burdening you and weighing you down. If it has been a while since reading the four types of weariness from the introduction to this retreat, pause and reread them now. Consider how your soul is responding to your felt weariness.

Imagine Jesus addressing you directly through Matthew 11:28-30. Sit with this image as long as possible, picturing yourself in the scene. Consider his promise, "You will find rest for your souls."

Psalm 42 offers many illustrations of the shape a soul might take. The psalmist describes a soul in despair and "cast down," and like a tornado "in turmoil within me" (Ps 42:5). There is also a soul that "thirsts" for God, parched and dehydrated (Ps 42:2).

Take a moment and visualize your soul's condition, and when you are ready, draw a picture representing the shape or state of your soul right now. If you brought clay or Play-Doh, you may use that to create a representation of your soul.

>}}}}⊛}}}{

Despite the origin of your weariness, God's solution is always the easy yoke that comes with Jesus. This yoke, this instrument of work, is formed for you specifically, and he will lay nothing ill-fitting or cumbersome on you. There are times and seasons in life where the yoke is well fitted, but we can bend under its weight—seasons like having several small children, a stage of illness or heavy grief, or a friend or community member in deep need. Perhaps you have picked up things along the way that you are not meant to carry. Perhaps the burden, even if a good fit for your life, feels heavy because you are trying to manage all its effects on your own. Talk to Jesus about these things and ask him what he might want to carry for you.

Is not this the fast that I choose:
　　to loose the bonds of wickedness,
　　to undo the straps of the yoke,
　to let the oppressed go free,
　　and to break every yoke? (Isaiah 58:6)

Questions for Journaling

- ✐ In the above Scripture, Jesus refers to the soul as weary and burdened. What shape is your soul in?
- ✐ What would it mean for this soul to find rest under the yoke of Jesus? What might it need?
- ✐ What yoke are you under? How is this revealed in the shape/state of your soul?
- ✐ What weight or bondage is keeping you from the easy yoke Jesus offers?

Give voice to all that comes up in you: expectations you put on yourself or those from others, duties, responsibilities, pain, hurt, and loss. This is not a time for fixing; this is simply receiving information about what is true and being willing to look at it with your friend Jesus close by.

CLOSING PRAYER

God, I thank you that the work you have for me is tied to you, and you will lay nothing heavy or ill-fitting on me. Give me discernment throughout this retreat to see what I am yoked or attached to other than you. I know that if we are joined together under your yoke, it will keep me close to you. Help me travel at your pace, seeing what you see, loving what you love, and resting when you rest. Amen.

EVENING

Weariness from Sin

OPENING SCRIPTURE—PSALM 139:23-24 NIV

Search me, God, and know my heart;
Test me and know my anxious thoughts.
See if there is any offensive way in me,
and lead me in the way everlasting.

OPENING PRAYER

Most holy and merciful Father:
We confess to you and to one another,
and to the whole communion of saints
in heaven and on earth,
that we have sinned by our own fault
in thought, word, and deed;
by what we have done, and by what we have left undone.

(Litany of Penitence, Ash Wednesday,
from the Book of Common Prayer 1979)

REFLECTION

On this first evening of retreat, let us consider the weariness from sin we may be carrying that we are tired of managing, hiding, or excusing. Let us confess our sins "in thought, word, and deed." Remember, as the psalmist says, "Search me, God." We will invite God to search our hearts to reveal sin; we do not search ourselves.

Take a few moments of silence to become acquainted with your breathing. Rest in God's presence. Invite the

Holy Spirit to search your heart. Write down everything that comes to mind after each section:

- "Search me, God, and know my heart": Where has your heart been, what has it treasured? What do you love? What have you wanted?

- "Test me and know my anxious thoughts": Invite God to search your mind. Where is there anxiety? What are your thoughts? Where have they gone astray, away from God?

- "See if there is any offensive way in me": In what ways have you grieved the heart of God? Your words? Your actions? Whatever bubbles up, let yourself see it; let God see it. Confess it and let it go.

- "And lead me in the way everlasting": What am I called to and how have I neglected that call? Where have I grown weary in my vocation, my relationships, my home, and my neighborhood? What have I left undone that you have called me to do?

Sit for a few moments in silence and ask the Holy Spirit to bring up anything else in your heart, things done or left undone, and confess it all to God. Now is not the time to double down on self-flagellation (such as, "I know I should have brought that family a casserole when they had their new baby. I feel terrible that I keep dodging my mother-in-law's phone calls. . . . I will do $x, y,$ and z to be better."). Prayer is not a place to try harder; it is a place to honestly unburden ourselves before God.

Read and receive these verses from 1 John as you prepare to close this time.

"Even if we feel guilty, God is greater than our feelings, and he knows everything" (1 John 3:20 NLT).

"If we confess our sins, he is faithful and just to forgive us our sins and to cleanse us from all unrighteousness" (1 John 1:9).

Consider a tangible expression of what it means to give your sin burden over to God, leaving it at the cross. What can you do externally that represents this internal reality?

CLOSING PRAYER

"Praise be to the Lord, to God our Savior, who daily bears our burdens"(Ps 68:19 NIV). Jesus, you bear the weight of my sin, you bear the weight of the yoke we carry together. Without you, I would be crushed, but you hold me up. Thank you for the gift of being able to be honest with you. Thank you for releasing me from the burden of my sin. You set my heart at rest in your presence. Amen.

＊＊＊＊❀＊＊＊＊

Close your time of prayer with a bow of reverence to God or simply place your hand to your chest, feeling your own heartbeat, as a gesture acknowledging God's care for you and presence with you.

Rest, eat a nutritious dinner, and maybe take a slow stroll around your new landscape. Practice being in your own body, if you have been rushed and busy. Practice seeing the scenery, the people, and the natural beauty of your surroundings.

COMPLINE

Read the prayer for compline.

> Keep watch, dear Lord, with those who work, or watch, or weep this night, and give your angels charge over those who sleep. Tend the sick, Lord Christ; give rest to the weary, bless the dying, soothe the suffering, pity the afflicted, shield the joyous; and all for your love's sake. Amen. (Book of Common Prayer 1979)

Spend five minutes looking through your journal, reflecting on all you have experienced today.

As your day draws to a close, meditate on these words of Jesus recorded in John 14:27, "Not as the world gives do I give to you. Let not your hearts be troubled, neither let them be afraid."

End your evening with a prayer of examen:

What was life-giving to you today? Where did you feel the wind at your back?

What was draining for you today? What felt heavy or difficult?

Journal or otherwise explore these with God.

Gather together all the parts of yourself and present them to God. Receive this blessing:

> In peace I will lie down and fall asleep, for you alone, O Lord, make me dwell in safety. O come and bless the Lord, all you servants of the Lord, who stand by day and night in the house of the Lord. Lift up your hands

to the holy place, and bless the Lord. May the all-powerful Lord grant us a restful night and a peaceful end. Amen.

}}}}}} DAY TWO {{{{{

Rest upon waking. Have coffee in bed or follow any other practice that feels luxurious or comforting as you prepare to rest in Jesus today.

PRAYER OF RECOLLECTION

Move through these three phases of prayer each morning on your retreat, taking as long as you need for each one. Consider incorporating this prayer into your rhythm of life after returning home.

1. ***Prayer of presentation.*** Dear God, here I am. I present myself to you as one who is holy and pleasing to you. I lay out the pieces of my life before you, and let you see all that is within me. I acknowledge the unilateral nature of your love; all action starts with you. When I come to prayer, I am entering into a conversation I did not start and do not sustain. I wake to a day I did not create, into a universe I do not uphold, into a life I did not earn, and into circumstances I cannot control. Awaken my soul to the reality that I can do nothing apart from you. Thank you, that you are always with me and that I am never alone (see Rom 12:1-2; 8:34; Heb 1:3; Jn 15:5; Mt 28:20).

2. ***Prayer of detachment.*** Dear God, I let go of anything I try to gain apart from you. I am not defined by my roles: a good or bad mother or father, sister or brother,

daughter or son, husband or wife, coworker, student, boss, or friend. These capacities do not define who I am, nor do health or sickness, poverty or wealth, success or failure, applause or slander. I detach from these roles— however vital and important, they are not at the core of who I am. In places where I have managed to be good, I count Christ more worthy than my success. In areas where I have failed, I ask forgiveness and let go of trying to make something of myself, proving myself to the world, or trying to earn your love, which is given freely (see Phil 3:7-8).

3. *Prayer of attachment.* Dear God, there is nothing you would not do and have not done to make me your own. I receive your mercy and grace. I was created for union with you, and by Jesus' sacrifice, I am saved from separation from you. At my center, I am in you and you are in me. I can only locate my true self in you. I am unrighteous on my own, but you are my righteousness. I am chaotic on my own, but you have given me the rightly ordered mind of Christ. Because you have attached me to yourself and will never let me go, I have full forgiveness, freedom, acceptance, and pardon from my sin, guilt, and shame. I am blameless in your sight. You delight in me and delight to co-labor with me in the unique, good work you have called me to. I am precious and irreplaceable to you. No matter the circumstance in which I find myself, I know that nothing comes to me that did not first pass through the cross. No matter what else is true of me in this life, at the center of my being is beloved belonging; I am a child

of God. There is nowhere I can run where you will not follow, nowhere I can hide where you will not find me. No matter how deep I go into my soul with you, I will find love, all the way down (see Col 1:22; Gal 2:20; Col 2:13-15; Rom 8:16; Ps 139:7-12).

Questions for Journaling

🖋 Which of these, if any, is difficult for your soul to receive?

🖋 Where are you feeling open to God today?

🖋 Which of these, if any, is hard for you to detach from?

🖋 What truths were you able to receive fully? Confess any unbelief.

🖋 Look back at the picture you drew yesterday representing the state of your soul. How does this picture illuminate the truths that are difficult for your soul to receive? What about this picture feels different for today?

MORNING

Weariness from Pain

OPENING SCRIPTURE—HEBREWS 12:1-2

Let us also lay aside every weight, and sin which clings so closely, and let us run with endurance the race that is set before us, looking to Jesus, the founder and perfecter of our faith.

OPENING PRAYER

God, you are always with me and will never leave me nor forsake me. You know when I sit and when I rise; all my ways are before you. You know every pain point in my life, even when I am unaware of it. Nothing is hidden from your sight. Be gracious to me in this time, as I open up places of pain within my heart. Set your hedge of love and protection behind me, before me, and on all sides. Amen.

REFLECTION

Notice the author of Hebrews separates "weight" and "sin." Last night we spent time confessing both our sin in what we had done and in what we had failed to do. We left it at the cross. But there can be other things that hinder our walk with Jesus that are not sin; they are "weights." Today we will look at weariness that comes from pain: the sin of others, pain points, wounds, trauma, grief, and even physical pain.

As I said earlier, when we address sin it's called repentance; when we address pain, it's called healing. We must leave room for this distinction because too often we struggle with shame, worry, fear, bad habits, self-protection, grabbiness, doubt, anger, addiction (I could go on) and label it as sin when perhaps it might be a pain point. We might be hurting. We make little progress spiritually, despite much confession, because pain cannot be repented of; it can only be healed.

Sit in silence for a few moments. Ask God to be present to you in this time, as you explore areas of pain. Repeat your prayer from Psalm 139 to allow God to search your heart and mind.

Questions for Journaling

🖉 Name any pain points in your life that need healing.
🖉 What would healing in this area look like to you?
🖉 What do you want to ask God for?

REFLECTION

For some, these are easy questions to answer; others are so weary and run down from long-term pain that it feels hard to access this part of themselves. If not much comes to mind, consider the list you made last night of sins to confess. Take my forgotten casserole or dodged phone call examples. Try to find something innocuous, something that makes you uneasy, or a benign habit you find yourself repeating. Some examples: Where do you find yourself longing to reach for your phone or other distractions to numb yourself? When during the day are you bored? What is going on during those parts of your day? Is there a particular place or person or activity you find annoying or perturbing, but you can't pinpoint why? Is there something you keep doing (or fail to do) that you wish you didn't? What is going on there?

Find a concrete example and spend ten minutes freewriting about it. Freewriting is just a stream of consciousness writing where you are not worried about grammatical errors. No one is reading this for clarity. Once you have a concrete pain point, person, or situation in mind, keep time for ten minutes. Do not set your pen down; even if you write "blah blah blah" for half a page, keep the momentum going.

Once ten minutes are up, look back at what you wrote. What do you notice? What surprised you?

What comfort is God offering you in the pain you are experiencing?

CLOSING PRAYER

God, I know that all the pain and hurt I have accumulated throughout my life cannot be summed up and dealt with on a forty-eight-hour retreat. Still, you are doing something here. You are unearthing things I did not see, and you have been faithful to "search and know" me. Thank you that nothing within me is hidden from your sight. Give me a sense of peace in this time as I have laid bare what has pained me. You are the Great Physician who longs to heal these fractured, fragmented parts of my soul. Guide me toward greater sources of support to help me unpack these wounds and receive your healing. Amen.

Note: If you find that the pain points that came up for you were new or overwhelming, consider reaching out for additional support. After debriefing this retreat with a pastor, friend, or spiritual director, it might be beneficial to take these areas of pain to a licensed therapist, as well.

AFTERNOON

Weariness from Doing Good

OPENING SCRIPTURE—GALATIANS 6:7-9

Do not be deceived: God is not mocked, for whatever one sows, that will he also reap. For the one who sows to his own flesh will from the flesh reap corruption, but the one who sows to the Spirit will from the Spirit reap eternal life. And let us not grow weary of doing good, for in due season we will reap, if we do not give up.

OPENING PRAYER

God, be with me as I open my heart to places where I have sown well, and to places where I have not. Place a steadfast spirit within me that I might not grow weary in the good work you have given me to do. Let me remember that in all my work, I am co-laboring with you for the good of your kingdom. Amen.

}}}}&}}}{

In this image Paul offers to the Galatians, he speaks of the harvest season, a time of joy when we reap the benefits of all our labors. But it's helpful to remember that even the harvest seasons of our lives require work. Bringing in loads of fruits or vegetables is time consuming and exhausting. And this is in a best-case scenario when we have planted rightly, when what we have sown in faith has borne fruit. Paul also alludes to the possibility that we can plant wrongly or in the flesh. These plants wither not from pest or storm but because they were not planted with Christ, sown in the Spirit.

Each season of life requires gardening tools. In spring we need a hoe to till the soil; in summer we need strong stakes to hold up leaning tomato plants; in fall we need a sturdy pair of clippers to prune; and in winter plenty of mulch to blanket plants and keep them safe from the cold.

Questions for Journaling

- What season is your soul in right now?
- What tools do you want to ask God for in this season of life?
- The plant that grows reveals the seed planted. What have you planted that has not grown the way you wanted it to?
- What have you planted that shows no signs of life?

REFLECTION

Take out a piece of paper. Divide it into two columns. On one side, write down all that you are aware of that you have sown in the flesh. Some if not many of these will likely be good things you've done, such as parenting, working, and serving by your own willpower. Ask God to reveal your good intentions in this. Receive God's compassion on the parts of you that try to do life on your own. On the other side, write down all you sow or aim to sow in the Spirit. Receive God's invitation to do all of your life with him. Write down all that comes to mind. Fold up this piece of paper as small as you can.

Take your piece of paper outside and, if appropriate, dig a hole to plant it in the dirt. If this is not possible, consider other ways to hand over this list to God, to "sow in the Spirit." Pay attention to how it feels to release these things to God. If you could imagine this mound of dirt five years in the future, what, metaphorically, might be in its place?

Consider a long walk or hike before dinner, sharing all that comes up in you as you walk with Jesus, speaking to him as one friend speaks to another. Take this verse with you and meditate on it as you go: "Consider him who endured such opposition from sinners, so that you will not grow weary and lose heart" (Heb 12:3 NIV). Think about places of opposition in your own life and opposition in the life of Jesus. What are some connection points? What might Jesus want to say to you about this?

As you walk, see if you can find items to gather that represent your soul in this season. If it's winter, consider a bouquet of dried foliage; if it's spring, perhaps bottle up some water nearby; if it's summer, gather stones or shells or sand; if it's fall, find a leaf to press into a book or trace its edges on paper. End this time by reiterating your intention to do all parts of this retreat with God.

....

EVENING

Between Two Kingdoms

OPENING SCRIPTURE—LUKE 9:62

Jesus said to him, "No one who puts his hand to the plow and looks back is fit for the kingdom of God."

OPENING PRAYER

Our Father, which art in heaven, Hallowed be thy name. Thy kingdom come, Thy will be done, in earth, as it is in heaven. Give us this day our daily bread. And forgive us our debts, as we forgive our debtors. And lead us not into temptation, but deliver us from evil: For thine is the kingdom, and the power, and the glory, for ever. Amen. (Mt 6:9-13 KJV)

REFLECTION

Read Luke 9:57-62, placing yourself in the story. (For a quick review, see the imaginative prayer section in chapter two.) Listen carefully to Jesus' responses and pay attention to what comes up in you. Read it again, sitting with the images provided in the story, and see what parallels come up from your own life.

Take a few moments to complete a "despair prayer" exercise, a phrase coined by Sybil MacBeth. At the top of the page write, "I will follow you, Lord; but let me first ..." (Lk 9:61).

Write down anything that causes your mind to wander, worry, or fret, drawing a bubble around each. Fill the page with all that comes to mind.

Once you have written down all that derails your intention to follow Jesus, see how you placed them on the paper. Are some bigger or smaller? How does it feel to see them fill the page? Ponder with God how each of these bubbles has the capacity to pull your soul in different directions.

In the center of the paper write an anchoring verse that feels meaningful to you now, or draw a picture or word that represents God at your center, despite the chaos around.

Go back to your bubbles and make them beautiful, coloring around the edges, perhaps connecting them to the center verse or idea, and praying through each of them. As you pray over each bubble, release it and let it float into God's care.

Consider the Luke 9 passage in conjunction with the imagery offered in Luke 17:32-33: "Remember Lot's wife. Whoever seeks to preserve his life will lose it, but whoever loses his life will keep it." Lot's wife was told not to look back while fleeing the land of Sodom. She did and suffered the consequences.

Questions for Journaling

- How have the worries, burdens, and cares you carry derailed you in your walk with Jesus?
- Where has your focus been? How has it kept you from peace, rest, and joy?
- What do you learn about Jesus through these interactions?
- What is God asking you to leave behind or let go of?
- What direction is Jesus calling you to travel in? What direction are you facing?

CLOSING PRAYER

"I have set the LORD always before me" (Ps 16:8). God, I set my mind, my heart, and my attention on you. Grant me focused endurance. I want to be in it with you for the long haul. I want to follow you and the ways of your kingdom. You know I am surrounded by distractions and carry a deep weariness within. Grant me grace to follow you. Sustain me in my weariness and let me not be derailed by lesser things. Amen.

COMPLINE

Read the prayer for compline:

> Keep watch, dear Lord, with those who work, or watch, or weep this night, and give your angels charge over those who sleep. Tend the sick, Lord Christ; give rest to the weary, bless the dying, soothe the suffering, pity the afflicted, shield the joyous; and all for your love's sake. Amen. (Book of Common Prayer 1979)

Spend five minutes reflecting on all you have experienced today by looking through your journal, considering the two images we have held on this retreat: the yoke Jesus offers—tethered to him, made to fit us well—and the image the author of Hebrews gives of Jesus "set before us" as the fixed location of our travels.

What stands out to you? What threads do you see now that you didn't earlier? What does God want to say to you about this?

End your evening with a prayer of examen:

What was life-giving to you today? Where did you feel the wind at your back?

What was draining for you today? What felt heavy or difficult?

Journal or otherwise explore these with God.

As your day draws to a close, meditate on these words of Jesus recorded in John 14:27 (NIV): "I do not give to you as the world gives. Do not let your hearts be troubled and do not be afraid."

Gather together all the parts of yourself and present them to God. Receive this blessing:

In peace I will lie down and fall asleep, for you alone, O Lord, make me dwell in safety. O come and bless the Lord, all you servants of the Lord, who stand by day and night in the house of the Lord. Lift up your hands to the holy place, and bless the Lord. May the all-powerful Lord grant us a restful night and a peaceful end. Amen.

⟫⟫⟫ DAY THREE ⟪⟪⟪

Rest on waking. Have coffee in bed or follow any other practice that feels luxurious or comforting as you prepare to rest in Jesus today.

PRAYER OF RECOLLECTION
Refer to day two.

....

MORNING

Weariness from Spiritual Bypassing

OPENING SCRIPTURE—EXODUS 20:21
The people remained at a distance, while Moses approached the thick darkness where God was.

OPENING PRAYER
God, I want to be with you where you are. While others might stay at a distance, in this retreat I have come up the mountain to be with you even if that means facing darkness. Let me have confidence in approaching you knowing that even "darkness is as light to you" (Ps 139:12 NIV). Amen.

REFLECTION
Paint or draw a picture that symbolizes the "thick darkness" where God dwells. How does it feel to draw near to this darkness? What is its shape, feel, color, and texture? How has it been for you to look at the darker aspects of your soul on this retreat?

Now that your body has rested for over twenty-four hours, where do you feel more open to engaging with emotions you were not open to at the beginning of your retreat? In what ways have you been expending energy negating, numbing, or distracting yourself from what you do not want to feel? How have you been able to attend to sadness, fear, guilt, or shame? Have you been able to come out of hiding and present yourself to God on this retreat? What parts of you remain resistant?

How did it feel to read in the introduction to this retreat that we often try to make our way *around* the darkness, when God beckons us to come *near* it with him (see Ex 20:21)? How does this fit with your view of God? What does it mean to you to approach God even if it means drawing near to the "thick darkness?"

It is said of Moses, "The LORD used to speak to Moses face to face, as a man speaks to his friend" (Ex 33:11).

Part of the issue with spiritual bypassing is a refusal to see things as they are. What in your life has had the effect of keeping you from seeing things as they are, keeping you in the dark—people, institutions, conversations, past hurts, etc.? What do you want to say to God about how you see yourself right now?

How do you think God sees you?

"But now [Jesus] has reconciled you by Christ's physical body through death to present you holy in his sight, without blemish and free from accusation" (Col 1:22 NIV). When God looks us in the face, we are somehow holy and blameless to him. How does this image make you feel? Spend some time with his image as you close this retreat, looking at the face of Jesus, seeing him as he is and asking what he sees in you.

Questions for Journaling

✎ What did you bring into this retreat with you?

✎ What are you leaving behind? Release all of these to the Lord and affirm who you are in him—beloved, free, delightful, celebrated adult child, and heir.

✎ Have you been able to turn your attention to God? What has that been like for you?

✎ What will you carry with you out of this retreat?

As you close this time, try to leave the last thirty minutes to an hour of your retreat as a time to remain in this posture of silence as you practice resting in God who loves you beyond measure. End by entrusting yourself to the God who sees, knows, and loves you completely.

As you transition into leaving your retreat, even as you pack up your belongings, leave time to do it slowly, mindfully, and in step with the Holy Spirit.

CLOSING PRAYER

Jesus, you are the good shepherd whose rod and staff comfort me. Your rod is your authority over evil, and your staff represents your willingness to confront darkness. Your rod and staff protect me in whatever dark places I might find myself. Even the darkness is as light to you. Seal by your Holy Spirit all that you did in my soul during this retreat. Be with me as I go and light the way home. Amen.

A BLESSING AS YOU GO

SERENITY PRAYER

God grant me the serenity
To accept the things I cannot change;
Courage to change the things I can;
And wisdom to know the difference.
Living one day at a time;
Enjoying one moment at a time;
Accepting hardships as the pathway to peace;
Taking, as He did, this sinful world
As it is, not as I would have it;
Trusting that He will make all things right
If I surrender to His Will;
So that I may be reasonably happy in this life
And supremely happy with Him
Forever and ever in the next. Amen.

8

FOR A TIME OF TRANSITION

✝

Every adult I know has experienced a season of transition. Some transitions hit us from the outside: the spouse quit, the company went under, or the doctor's office called with news. An event has altered the timeline of our lives into what happened before and what will come after. Other times we embrace transition. We sense something new within us longs to be born, or that our old ways of living no longer serve us as they used to. The page in our story is turning over quietly and surely, and cannot be postponed. Change is coming even if we do not know when or how; we can smell it on the wind. What once was is gone and what is to be has not yet revealed itself.

In the Scriptures, God often calls people in a new direction or a new way of living against the backdrop of a desert landscape. God spoke to Abram in the desert with a starry sky, promising descendants outnumbering all he could see (see Gen 15:5). God called Moses out of herding sheep and into herding his people to freedom from a flaming bush on the "west side of the wilderness" at Horeb (Ex 3:1).

We know David wrote some of his most heartfelt poetry fleeing from his oppressors and hiding in deserted caves. The apostle Paul tells the Galatians about his necessary journey into the wilderness. Describing his conversion he says, "I did not immediately consult with anyone; nor did I go up to Jerusalem to those who were apostles before me, but I went away into Arabia" (Gal 1:16-17). He experienced the solitude of wilderness for three years with God as a transition from his old life of persecuting Christians to his new life of shepherding them. These faithful ones know what it is like to inhabit the land in between: they could not go back and did not know the way forward. For years and sometimes decades they endured the discomfort of transition. As they wandered as exiles on the earth, they learned to find their home in God.

This liminal space, this wilderness, is a necessary passageway for spiritual growth and God's chosen method at hinge points in our lives—a method many of us avoid. When we cannot see what is around the next bend, when the diagnosis, loss, or wound leaves us in this middle place, we naturally avoid it. We have mastered any number of ways of escapism: booze, sex, media, people, work, or the constant hum and ding of the computer we carry in our pockets. It does not take much energy or foresight to silence the cricket chirp of our own soul. We do not yet see that the pathway to freedom is often through miles and miles of hot sand.

The Israelites' movement out of Egypt as slaves into the Promised Land of God took a process of forty years. Jesus modeled his first retreat after their wandering, rehearsing in his body all that was lost and all that was found. The

Israelites had been so habituated by generations of slavery that they could not conceptualize themselves as free people overnight. Their souls needed retraining from decades spent not as unique, beloved sons and daughters, but as property—dispensable, interchangeable property. What had to be re-trained, re-formed in the desert were their souls, their worth, and their identity. This teaches us something about the nature of transitions: they take a long time, and what often results is not just a new location but a whole new version of ourselves.

God used Paul's three years, David's thirteen years, and the Israelites' forty years to make their souls as free as their bodies were. This tells us that time is profoundly necessary in forming our souls toward freedom. It takes time for us to change, to grow, to be shaped by God's love. Many of us at the cusp of the wilderness would say, "Give me the GPS coordinates, God. I can take it from here." We would choose destination over transformation every time, but God loves us too much to deliver our bodies somewhere new and leave our souls as they are. God knows what we are still learning: no matter where we go, we bring ourselves with all our problems and baggage.

There is a great and mysterious mercy in the desert. Streams of living water are waiting to be found if you know where to look for them. When the path seems blocked by a large boulder, the desert reveals that it hides a gushing spring of water. Where all seems dry and lifeless, God can produce a fountain. When food is scarce, God causes it to fall from the sky. God leads us into the wilderness to speak tenderly to us (see Hos 2:14). In these painful, dry, and desolate places, we will find we can hear his voice, sense his presence, and experience his providence better than in lush conditions. May we have eyes to see and ears to hear that God often brings us into wild places to set us free.

﹥﹥﹥﹥ DAY ONE ﹤﹤﹤﹤

Begin by reviewing chapter five, the "Arrival Guide."

....

AFTERNOON

Holy Discontent

OPENING SCRIPTURE—HOSEA 2:14-15

Therefore, behold, I will allure her,
  and bring her into the wilderness,
  and speak tenderly to her.
And there I will give her her vineyards.

OPENING PRAYER

Thank you, God, that nothing takes you by surprise. You know all the days of my life before one of them comes to be. I trust you to guide me in this wilderness I find myself in. Amen.

REFLECTION

Begin this time of prayer with a short walk outdoors to gather a "wilderness bouquet." Meditating on the opening Scripture, look for the alluring beauty of God where you are. Gather organic elements around you, preferably native plants, weeds, or grasses. Even if the stem looks dead or dying, gather it up. See how many different elements you can gather, perhaps tying them together or putting them in a glass or vase.

Keeping your wilderness bouquet in sight, consider where you are resisting this transition period in your life, especially if it is unwanted or has taken you by surprise. Talk with God about all that preceded your travels into the wilderness. What places feel beautiful, as if God brought (allured) you here? Where do you feel thrust out into the wilderness against your will?

There is something special about the desert landscape; perhaps it's the lack of distractions and noises found in cities full of bustling people. God uses the desert setting to deepen conversations with those he calls to himself. In the Genesis account of Abraham and Sarah, the mother and father of all Israelites, lies a disturbing story about Sarah's slave, Hagar. Sarah forces Hagar to have sex with her husband Abraham, and when she conceives, she is so overcome with jealousy

> *Transition(s) of the heart often come slowly. We look back and in retrospect see that something has grown gradually in our heart, perhaps a holy discontent, and we know that in good conscience we need to ask how to best navigate this transition with a faithful and hopeful response.*
>
> GORDON T. SMITH

that she beats Hagar. Hagar flees her abusers and finds herself lost in the desert. "The angel of the LORD" meets her there and asks, "Where have you come from and where are you going?" (Gen 16:7-8).

Read Genesis 16:1-8. Place yourself in this story, imagining the angel addressing you directly. As you read it a second time, think back on the journey that brought you

to this retreat: the morning chaos, packing, and preparing. Think back to the past week or month.

Questions for Journaling

- Where have you been?
- Where are you going?
- How did God prepare you and lead you into this time with him?
- Where has your soul been today, this week, this month, this year?
- Talk to God about the lack of answers and clarity in your own time of transition. What do you sense his posture is like toward you as you speak these truths to him?

CLOSING PRAYER

If this time of transition was something you did choose (or at least saw coming), did it start with a "holy discontent"? For your closing prayer, name with God all that comes up in you as holy discontent. Tell him, too, what you hope might be your faithful and hopeful response. Close your time of prayer with a bow of reverence to God or simply place your hand to your chest, feeling your own heartbeat, as a gesture acknowledging God's care for you and presence with you.

⋙⋙❖⋘⋘

Rest, eat a nutritious dinner, and maybe take a slow stroll around your new landscape. Practice being in your body, if you have been rushed and busy. Find a spot for your wilderness bouquet and contemplate the scenery, the people, and the natural beauty of your surroundings.

EVENING

Turning Aside

Earth's crammed with heaven,
And every common bush afire with God;
But only he who sees takes off his shoes,
The rest sit around and pluck blackberries.

OPENING PRAYER

When you go on retreat you choose to respond to the movements of God in your life. You are one who sees and takes off your shoes. You are here to rest in the presence of a holy God. Take a moment to solidify that intention within you as you open to God in prayer.

OPENING SCRIPTURE—EXODUS 3:1-6

Now Moses was keeping the flock of his father-in-law, Jethro, the priest of Midian, and he led his flock to the west side of the wilderness and came to Horeb, the mountain of God. And the angel of the LORD appeared to him in a flame of fire out of the midst of a bush. He looked, and behold, the bush was burning, yet it was not consumed. And Moses said, "I will turn aside to see this great sight, why the bush is not burned." When the LORD saw that he turned aside to see, God called to him out of the bush, "Moses, Moses!" And he said, "Here I am." Then he said, "Do not come near; take your sandals off your feet, for the place on which you are standing is holy ground." And he said, "I am the God of your father, the God of Abraham, the God of Isaac, and the God of Jacob." And Moses hid his face, for he was afraid to look at God.

Read this Scripture lectio divina style, reading it several times and pausing between to let God speak in whatever way he wishes. This is not a time for study but a time to be refreshed and nourished by the living Word of God given to you. (Review the lectio divina instructions in chapter two.)

In the second reading, reflect on a word or phrase that shimmered or stood out to you. Give yourself a few minutes to do this. Then ask God, "How does this connect with my life today? What do I need to know or be or do?"

In the third reading, prepare yourself to respond to God. Moses, in the wilderness, heard God's call because he went aside to the burning bush. In retreat, you are stepping off the beaten path, saying yes to God's invitation to rest and solitude. Once God saw Moses "turn aside," then he called out to him. Explore with God this image of Moses, alone, perhaps at night, in the middle of the desert. Imagine yourself there, in solitude and quiet.

Questions for Journaling

- Are you willing to fully give yourself to time away with God, to step off the beaten path, to see "this great sight" God is doing, even if it doesn't make sense or follow your plan? Explore with God your desire to be alone with him but also any resistance you are feeling to it. Be as honest as you can.
- What does God want to say to you?
- Explore doubt. What keeps you from turning aside?

In the fourth reading, simply rest. Do as you are led. Is God asking you to wait on him, hand something over, or rest more deeply in him? Sit in the loving presence of God—the One who beckons you to come away with him.

REFLECTION

What gentle promptings do you have that God might be leading you in a new direction?

Think through your fears, concerns, and worries about leaving the road less traveled and stepping onto this narrow path with God. How do you want to respond to this call in a tangible way? How can you respond externally in a way that represents this internal reality?

CLOSING PRAYER

God, I want to come away and be with you where you are. Help me to attend to what you are doing. Let me not miss the burning bushes around me. Thank you for calling me onto the narrow path, the road less traveled, and even if I feel lonely here, I am truly never alone. You are always with me. Amen.

COMPLINE

As you pray compline, picture again the image of Hagar in the desert. After her interaction with the angel of God, she gave God a name. Hagar is famous for being the first female ever to give a name to God in Scripture. The name she gave him was El Roi, the God Who Sees: "I have now seen the One who sees me" (Gen 16:13 NIV).

In this closing prayer of the night, hold the image of God as a God who looks after you. He watches over those who work or watch or weep. His eyes are on us all, caring for us, tending to our needs even as we are helplessly, vulnerably, unproductively asleep. Release yourself to God. Release your loved ones to God. Tell him if it is difficult to be away from them on this retreat. Entrust them to his watchful care. Release your cares and worries to God, entrusting yourself to the God who looks after you.

Read the prayer for compline.

Keep watch, dear Lord, with those who work, or watch, or weep this night, and give your angels charge over those who sleep. Tend the sick, Lord Christ; give rest to the weary, bless the dying, soothe the suffering, pity the afflicted, shield the joyous; and all for your love's sake. Amen. (Book of Common Prayer 1979)

Spend five minutes looking through your journal, reflecting on all you have experienced today.

End your evening with a prayer of examen:

What was life-giving to you today? Where did you feel the wind at your back?

What was draining for you today? What felt heavy or difficult?

Journal or otherwise explore these with God.

Receive this blessing:

In peace I will lie down and fall asleep, for you alone, O Lord, make me dwell in safety. O come and bless the Lord, all you servants of the Lord, who stand by day and night in the house of the Lord. Lift up your hands to the holy place, and bless the Lord. May the all-powerful Lord grant us a restful night and a peaceful end. Amen.

))))) DAY TWO (((((

Rest upon waking. Have coffee in bed or follow any other practice that feels luxurious or comforting as you prepare to rest in Jesus today.

PRAYER OF RECOLLECTION

Move through these three phases of prayer each morning on your retreat, taking as long as you need for each one. Consider incorporating this prayer into your rhythm of life after returning home.

1. *Prayer of presentation:* Dear God, here I am. I present myself to you as one who is holy and pleasing to you. I lay out the pieces of my life before you, and let you see all that is within me. I acknowledge the unilateral nature of your love; all action starts with you. When I come to prayer, I am entering into a conversation I did not start and do not sustain. I wake to a day I did not create, into a universe I do not uphold, into a life I did not earn, and into circumstances I cannot control. Awaken my soul to the reality that I can do nothing apart from you. Thank you, that you are always with me and that I am never alone (see Rom 12:1-2; 8:34; Heb 1:3; Jn 15:5; Mt 28:20).

2. *Prayer of detachment:* Dear God, I let go of anything I try to gain apart from you. I am not defined by my roles: a good or bad mother or father, sister or brother, daughter or son, husband or wife, coworker, student, boss, or friend. These capacities do not define who I am, nor do health or sickness, poverty or wealth, success or

failure, applause or slander. I detach from these roles—however vital and important; they are not at the core of who I am. In places where I have managed to be good, I count Christ more worthy than my success. In areas where I have failed, I ask forgiveness and let go of trying to make something of myself, proving myself to the world, or trying to earn your love, which is given freely (see Phil 3:7-8).

3. *Prayer of attachment.* Dear God, there is nothing you would not do and have not done to make me your own. I receive your mercy and grace. I was created for union with you, and by Jesus' sacrifice, I am saved from separation from you. At my center, I am in you and you are in me. I can only locate my true self in you. I am unrighteous on my own, but you are my righteousness. I am chaotic on my own, but you have given me the rightly ordered mind of Christ. Because you have attached me to yourself and will never let me go, I have full forgiveness, freedom, acceptance, and pardon from my sin, guilt, and shame. I am blameless in your sight. You delight in me and delight to co-labor with me in the unique, good work you have called me to. I am precious and irreplaceable to you. No matter the circumstance in which I find myself, I know that nothing comes to me that did not first pass through the cross. No matter what else is true of me in this life, at the center of my being is beloved belonging; I am a child of God. There is nowhere I can run where you will not follow, nowhere I can hide where you will not find me. No matter how deep I go into my soul with you, I

will find love, all the way down (see Col 1:22; Gal 2:20; Col 2:13-15; Rom 8:16; Ps 139:7-12).

Questions for Journaling

- ✐ Which of these, if any, is difficult for your soul to receive?
- ✐ Where are you feeling open to God today?
- ✐ Which of these, if any, is hard for you to detach from?
- ✐ What truths were you able to receive fully? Confess any unbelief.

....

MORNING

Waiting on God

OPENING SCRIPTURE—PSALM 62:1

For God alone my soul waits.

OPENING PRAYER

God, I wait on you, for you alone refresh my soul. Help me to fully release all the other things I think I am waiting for: people, vocations, future plans, and milestones. I can only access your mercies for today; I cannot claim tomorrow's mercies (Lam 3:23). I take this day to fully wait on you to do in my life what only you can do. Amen.

REFLECTION

That is why waiting does not diminish us, any more than waiting diminishes a pregnant mother. We are enlarged in the waiting. We, of course, don't see what is enlarging us. But the longer we wait, the larger we become, and the more joyful our expectancy.

Meanwhile, the moment we get tired in the waiting, God's Spirit is right alongside us helping us along. (Rom 8:23-26 MSG)

Our dominant social narrative is one of certainty, of five- or ten-year plans, and of safety and personal happiness above all. This is difficult for someone in the desert wandering in circles. Our culture does not prioritize stillness, suffering, waiting, and uncertainty—all wilderness requirements. We want to get over it, get there, and get there fast. Waiting, pausing, resting, and retreating in a time of transition seem antithetical to our culture's value of hurrying on to the next thing. But what is next often cannot be revealed until we slow down. In a time of transition, the greatest gift we can give our souls, and often the thing we want least, is to wait. The great challenge for us who find ourselves in this in-between land is to stay put when it is uncomfortable, unnerving, and disorienting. God wants to do work in the wilderness he cannot do in any other place. The wilderness is truly holy ground.

Parker Palmer says,

The soul is like a wild animal—tough, resilient, savvy, self-sufficient, and yet exceedingly shy. If we want to see a wild animal, the last thing we should do is to go crashing through the woods, shouting for the creature to come out. But if we are willing to walk quietly in the woods and sit silently for an hour or two at the base of a tree, the creature we are waiting for may well emerge, and out of the corner of an eye we will catch a glimpse of the precious wildness we seek.

Consider going outdoors for the remainder of this morning's session. As you journal and close in prayer, pay attention to what is happening around you as you are still. What emerges that you might have otherwise missed? What do you notice about the creation around you that is also waiting; groaning in expectancy (see Rom 8:22)?

Questions for Journaling

- Now that you have paused your body for almost twenty-four hours, examine how you feel. Restless? Tired? Afraid? At peace?
- In what areas are you having difficulty waiting on God? What do you most want to be cut short in your circumstances right now?
- Do you have any sense of being "enlarged in the waiting"? Where do you feel pressure at your growing edge?
- How do you normally respond to waiting? How are you responding now?

CLOSING PRAYER

In waiting, we realize we are both receptive and helpless. We cannot enact change in our own lives. We can do nothing on our own. We need God desperately. One way to tune in to this desperation is through prayers of other desperate people in Scripture. One that I often find myself returning to in seasons of transition comes from a prayer prayed by Hannah to God. Hannah was in a season of deep soul wilderness and had finally come to a place of full surrender to God.

Crushed in soul, Hannah prayed to GOD and cried and cried—inconsolably. Then she made a vow:

> Oh God-of-the-Angel-Armies,
> If you'll take a good, hard look at my pain,
> If you'll quit neglecting me and go into action for me
> By giving me a son,
> I'll give him completely, unreservedly to you.
> (1 Sam 1:10-11 MSG)

This prayer encompasses what I experience in the desert when I am at my most desperate. I am aware of my pain but not convinced God is, or that he cares. I feel, if I am my most honest, neglected by God. Part of me is aware that he could pull me from the desert at any moment if he wished. I am tempted most in transition seasons to doubt God's love and provision.

Hannah was desperate for a child and knew she could not accomplish pregnancy on her own. She needed God desperately. So she calls him by the most powerful name she can think of: God of Angel Armies; Lord of Heavenly Hosts. She knows that in the wilderness her only hope is for God to go into action on her behalf. All her hope is in him.

Use Hannah's prayer as your own breath prayer for at least five breaths: inhale on the first line, exhale on the second. Sit in this open, dependent posture for as long as you like, soaking in God's love for you and his great care for you.

Become aware of where you are waiting on God and most longing for his intervention.

God of Angel Armies (inhale)

Go into action for me. (exhale)

Release to God any pain points or disbelief. Spend a few moments with your hands and heart open, resting in dependence on a God who loves you, sees you, and longs to show you compassion. As you go about your morning and early afternoon, aim to stay in this place of peaceful presence, simply *being* with God.

....

AFTERNOON

Longing for God

OPENING SCRIPTURE—ISAIAH 30:18

Therefore the LORD waits to be gracious to you, and therefore he exalts himself to show mercy to you. (ESV)

So the LORD must wait for you to come to him so he can show you his love and compassion. (NLT)

Yet the LORD longs to be gracious to you; therefore he will rise up to show you compassion. (NIV)

OPENING PRAYER

God, be with me as I explore your nature as a compassionate God. There are places within me that may readily agree with this. There are places in me that are deeply resistant to this. Even in my resistance, you wait for me, even long for me to come to you. Thank you for loving me this way. Amen.

REFLECTION

Spend a few moments calling to mind a time when you distinctly felt the compassion of God in a situation in your life. Take all the time you need to get very clear on this experience, writing it out in story form if that is helpful. Where were you, who were you with, what were you doing, what life stage were you in? Call to mind as many details as possible, down to what season it was in and what you were wearing. What were the smells, the sights, the sounds?

Once you have this moment as clear as you can get it, spend some time engaging with it with your art materials. Draw a portion of the event, or the whole scene. Who was God to you in this moment? (Kind, Good Father, Deliverer, Sustainer?) What name do you want to give him? Find a rock or something in nature that represents it, and paint this word/name on it, or create a 3D version of the scene with organic elements outdoors. Be creative in engaging with this event in a tactile way.

Questions for Journaling

- How have you experienced, or not experienced, the compassion of God?
- What comes up in you when you picture God *longing* for you?
- Are there any places in you that feel resistant to God's compassion? What are they?
- Where have you been resisting God's invitation to wander, to wait, to be still?
- If your longing had a voice, what would it want to say to God right now?

Spend the afternoon receiving God's compassion for you by nourishing and caring for your body. Consider this God who waits on you and wants to know you. Not only that—he is a God who wants *you* to know what is in your own heart. Ponder the intimacy of this, that God longs for us to come to him. God sees all we are, all we have been, and loves us enough to invite us into this knowing too. His love is enough to sustain our self-knowledge, no matter how painful the revelations. If God wants to show you something, maybe a way you have resisted waiting in the wilderness process, let him show you. Rest in this compassionate God who knows you and invites you to know yourself.

CLOSING PRAYER

Thank you, God, that you never tire of waiting for me to come to you. Your love for me begins and ends with you. It is unilateral, pointing in my direction all the time. Let me rest in your one-sided love for me today. Amen.

....

EVENING

The Hidden Heart

OPENING SCRIPTURE—DEUTERONOMY 8:2

You shall remember the whole way that the LORD your God has led you these forty years in the wilderness, that he might humble you, testing you to know what was in your heart, whether you would keep his commandments or not.

OPENING PRAYER

God, you have been faithful to lead me to this place. Give me eyes to see how you have been present to me in all things. Give me ears to hear your voice and instruction. Give me a heart to know and love you more. Amen.

REFLECTION

Our actions display our hearts; they show us what is hidden in our souls. God tested the Israelites for forty years not so that he would know what was in their hearts (spoiler: he already knew) but that *they* might know their own hearts. The Israelites, for their part, treated this transition as if it were a burden to bear or a plot to kill them. They grumbled and complained. They accused Moses of trying to kill them by taking them out of Egypt. "Is it because there are no graves in Egypt that you have taken us away to die in the wilderness? . . . It would have been better for us to serve the Egyptians than to die in the wilderness" (Ex 14:11-12). God used the season of transition to expose what was in the hearts of the Israelites: anger, grumbling, confusion, thinking the worst of God, lack of faith, despair. These seem to be normal human responses to transition.

What has God exposed in your heart during this time of transition? Anger, fear, anxiety, trust? Bring these things to God.

In his book *Run with the Horses*, Eugene Peterson explores the clear certainties found in the Egyptian social life and landscape. He argues that Egypt was "clear" architecturally; the geometric magnitude of the pyramids meant to expel fear of death. "Egypt was clear socially," he goes on. "Everyone's place was defined hierarchically. . . . The diminishment of people was compensated for by the clarity of knowing where they stood." He also explains the clarity of the Egyptian theology. "The unseen was translated into the seen. All gods were made into images. Everything that might have been more than human was reduced to what was less than human: the cat, the hawk, the hyena, the bull, the ibis were the god-images of the Egyptians. . . . All wonder was eliminated." Peterson goes on to contrast the Egyptian clarity with the faith required to follow Yahweh, explaining that it's not as if there are no clarities in the life of faith but that these "clarities develop from within. They cannot be imposed from without. They cannot be hurried."

Pause with this and explore your own lack of clarity in this time of transition.

Later in the same Deuteronomy passage it says, "Your clothing did not wear out on you and your foot did not swell these forty years" (Deut 8:4). Allow the Holy Spirit to bring to mind ways in which God has sustained you in this time of transition.

Questions for Journaling

- How do you feel about your own lack of clarity in this season? Angry with God? Confused? Trusting? Numb?
- What do you want to say to God about your response to this transition season in your life?
- Where has God sustained you, perhaps unexpectedly?
- Where is God developing clarity from within?

CLOSING PRAYER

Thank you, God, Lord of heaven and earth, that you hide yourself from the proud but reveal yourself to those humble enough to seek you. Thank you for your presence, which is faithful to guide me. May your will be done in my life. Amen.

COMPLINE

Read the prayer for compline.

Keep watch, dear Lord, with those who work, or watch, or weep this night, and give your angels charge over those who sleep. Tend the sick, Lord Christ; give rest to the weary, bless the dying, soothe the suffering, pity the afflicted, shield the joyous; and all for your love's sake. Amen. (Book of Common Prayer 1979)

Spend five minutes looking through your journal, reflecting on all you have experienced today.

Compline is about God seeing you, caring for you, and holding all you care about as you rest.

Consider writing your own version of a compline prayer, given where you have journeyed with God today. Ask God to keep watch over all your concerns, worries, expectations, and fears.

>}}}⟩⟨⟩}}}⟨

Receive this blessing:

In peace I will lie down and fall asleep, for you alone, O Lord, make me dwell in safety. O come and bless the Lord, all you servants of the Lord, who stand by day and night in the house of the Lord. Lift up your hands to the holy place and bless the Lord. May the all-powerful Lord grant us a restful night and a peaceful end. Amen.

⟫⟫⟫ DAY THREE ⟨⟨⟨⟨

Rest upon waking. Have coffee in bed or follow any other practice that feels luxurious or comforting as you prepare to rest in Jesus today.

PRAYER OF RECOLLECTION

Refer to day two.

....

MORNING

A God Who Makes a Way

Note: There might be a temptation this morning to begin to worry about and prepare for going home. Try to mark off at least a section of your morning for quiet reflection before checking out or heading home. Keep this morning's time sacred and off-limits, as your mind wants to begin preparations for what's next. After the benediction, pack up slowly and mindfully, carrying the gentle rhythms you began on retreat home with you.

OPENING SCRIPTURE—ISAIAH 43:19-21

> *I will make a way in the wilderness*
> *and rivers in the desert. . . .*
> *For I give water in the wilderness,*
> *rivers in the desert,*
> *to give drink to my chosen people,*
> *the people whom I formed for myself*
> *that they might declare my praise.*

OPENING PRAYER

God, would you make a way where there is no way in the wilderness of my heart? In the places where I am blocked or resistant, may your gentle presence ebb and flow, moving where it wants to go. I open to you in this time; may your Spirit move as you will. Amen.

REFLECTION

Often in times of unknowing, in liminal, transitional seasons, what we want most is answers. God rarely offers those particulars. Instead, he does something unexpected; he makes "a way." The image we are given is one of water springing up in the wilderness, of it dripping and flowing in rivulets, making a path where previously there was none. "The way" often involves us walking by faith on a path that did not exist before we began traveling it with God.

As you reflect on these things, bring a glass of water outside with you. If you are near a body of water, you may want to interact differently, but begin by pouring water onto the ground, over a rock, or into a hole in the ground. Pay attention to the ways of water, how it always gravitates to lower ground. What does this say to you about how God's Spirit makes its way in your soul? How is God's Spirit and word sinking into deeper places within you over the course of this retreat?

Questions for Journaling

✐ Where is God calling you to walk a path that is unknown to you? How do you feel about being the one to forge this path?

⌀ What is your reaction to the slow growth of soul transformation? Frustration? Self-condemnation? Peace?

⌀ What parts of yourself have been enlarged in waiting?

⌀ What rooms and spaces in your soul have grown, even on this retreat? Do they have names, shapes, or colors?

⌀ What did you bring into this retreat with you and what are you leaving behind?

CLOSING PRAYER

God, your living water is always moving, filling in the gaps and crevices of my soul. You are always seeking deeper ground within me. Help me in my places of resistance, the barriers I put in place, to keep what is "mine" from what is "yours." Let the water of your Spirit flow in my life, taking up more and more space; let me not fill it up with lesser things. I welcome the enlarging and strengthening work you are doing within me in unseen places (see Eph 3:16). This is your work, not my own. God, by your Holy Spirit set your seal on this time of retreat; let it be preserved in my soul, in the secret place where only you dwell. Amen.

A BLESSING AS YOU GO

PSALM 52:8-9

But I am like a green olive tree
   in the house of God.
I trust in the steadfast love of God
   forever and ever.
I will thank you forever,
   because you have done it.

FOR ONE WHO IS GRIEVING

✝

If you are considering this retreat, most likely you have lost something. Grief comes in many forms: loss of a job, loss of identity, loss of a person—perhaps one you thought you could not live without. Grief comes in waves, both big and small, throughout our lives. We often minimize the smaller griefs, letting them pile atop one another until one day we wonder why it feels hard to breathe. The larger griefs tend to take us by surprise, as if we never thought they would come, a wave crashing without warning and threatening to drown us whole.

It is not advisable to spend time alone in solitude and silence in the early, disorienting days of a major grief episode. I take my cues from the Jewish mystics and thinkers who adhere to the practice of sitting shiva when a community member has died. They grieve as a corporate event. The bereaved are not allowed to be alone, not even for a moment in those early days of grief, where every mirror is covered, and the table is continually piled high with food from neighbors. For seven days the bereaved are surrounded, and even after this initial stage, checked on daily, with formal liturgies and corporate prayers recited during the first year of loss. The Jewish model of engaging with grief requires constant presence with the bereaved, which is rich with wisdom.

There comes a time, however, whether the grief is large or small, when pieces of it are ready to be attended to. Grief often provides a catalyst, a breaking, in which the person before the incident and the person after split into two different entities. We shatter in grief, the pieces of ourselves buckling and breaking, shard upon shard. We might still be going about our daily business looking whole to an outside observer, but inside we have fractured into a million pieces.

It is these pieces that ask to be attended to, in the right time, in the presence of God. In grief we have become alien to ourselves, a broken puzzle whose pieces do not fit together as they did before. We are not yet at the stage of rebuilding; we are only at the stage of seeing the pieces for what they are and naming them properly.

A friend of mine was widowed recently, and we spent a morning together celebrating that she learned to fix a leak under her bathroom sink. I had no idea how to do it, so I marveled at her new skill. But once we sat with this joy, the tears came too. We named this tiny part of what she is forced to do, who she is forced to be without her husband. She is forced to care for herself in this small-but-significant way. She no longer has him as a partner through life, in the big things and the small. This is its own grief and deserves to be named, recognized, held, and handed over to God.

Grief manifests itself differently depending on the loss. There are so many endings we cannot anticipate and do not

know how to release. We look at our grown kids at gradu-
ations or weddings, and we wonder, *When was the last time
he held my hand to cross the street? When was the last time I
tucked him into bed at night? I know there was a last, I just
didn't know it was coming. If I had known the last time I would
shampoo her hair in the tub or hold her on my hip, I may have
held on longer.* Our minds tug at the corners for memories
we cannot conjure up, trying and failing to name those
"lasts." We are left with the weight of moments we cannot
name or properly grieve. All the "lasts" we can name absorb
the weight of all the "lasts" we cannot, and perhaps that is
why they feel so heavy.

We hold each puzzle piece of our grief up to the light. We
let it be what it is. We name it properly in the presence of
God. We say what is true—with him. We expose our anger,
our dismay, our frustration. This often happens long after
we've left the casseroles and community behind. Alone on
retreat we do not have to find the good in all things. We do
not have to explain the diagnoses or try to give language
to the abrupt end to the engagement that we ourselves still
don't understand. We do not have to tell people how they
can help us or wonder why they don't ask. Mostly, we do
not have to tidy up our circumstances and make them more
palatable. God requires none of these.

Instead, he takes up residence and sits cross-legged on the
floor with us. He holds on to us as we weep. He sets a table
for when we are ready to eat. He tucks the covers around us
when we cannot get out of bed. Jesus of Nazareth allowed
all grief, all shame, all disorientation, all loneliness, all vio-
lence, all unfairness, all death and pain and sadness to flow

through his body on the cross. He absorbed it all. In a sense, all we are left with are the aftershocks.

But these aftershocks can cause damage. They can form foundational cracks in our faith, and when left unattended, become a breeding ground for anger, numbing, and despair. If we do not—at some point in our grief journey—face the reality of God in it, we build our lives on a cracked slate. And this is the foundational truth that grief makes us face: God could have prevented our loss. God, as we know him, is infinite, all-powerful, all-knowing. The term our creeds have used throughout the centuries is *sovereign*. God is also good. There is no evil in him, and his posture toward us is love. In grief, at the bottom of the well of our sorrow, we must face this awful tension: How can God be both good and sovereign? Why didn't God stop this from happening? Is he unable? Unwilling? Both? Where was God in this loss? This is where we begin.

Grief is terribly disorienting, often like a map without a legend. I like the visual of maps because grief, in my experience, is at least two things: One, it seems there are one million paths one could take, especially at the beginning. And two, we must travel these paths (not merely notice them) to find true healing. Following these paths where they take us is an integral part of the grief work. We grieve not only the loss of someone or something but all the implications of those losses on our body, our family, our comforts, the rhythm of our lives, what it might mean for our future . . . the list goes on, like branches on a tree or rivulets of water. Grief is messy, like trying to fit slime into a container; it just seeps into every crevice. It gets everywhere, infiltrating everything.

To be with our grief is to give it our attention. This is difficult in a culture that prizes getting past, getting ahead, and moving forward. It is difficult to wade into pain without our usual distractions and numbing devices. In grief, our bodies are often the canaries in the coal mines. We feel antsy, sick, uneasy, achy. We come down with frequent illness, chronic fatigue, and brain fog. Once, in a season of deep grief, after a bout of bronchitis, pneumonia, and a urinary tract infection, I was diagnosed with shingles. The body has a way of getting our attention when we do not want to give it.

Miriam Greenspan says, "The dark emotions are attention-grabbers, goading us into awareness. They're like young children: If you attend to them, they reward you. If you don't, prepare for trouble. They have their ways of letting you know they need your attention." When you allow yourself to lament, you assent to the grief that wants to be noticed within you.

The Psalms are often called the prayer book for God's people, and the majority of the psalms contain lament. Lament psalms express pain and grief. They often ask for God's help and sometimes note a felt absence. These are prayers of God's faithful prayed throughout the ages, over and over throughout the year. A good antidote to the loneliness that often accompanies grief is praying the Psalms, as you can be assured someone, somewhere in the world, is praying along with you, making this retreat a good one to follow in a monastic or prayerful community. The book of Psalms is also the book Jesus quoted the most. He was a man "acquainted with grief" (Is 53:3), and he has given us much room and grace to explore it. The Psalms offer an invaluable guide to partner with Jesus as we wade into the murky depths of grief.

In my deepest seasons of grief, when I am not able to do much, I will pray a lament psalm. If the exercises or prompts feel like too much in this season for you, simply read the included psalm as the opening prayer for each session. Praying a single psalm aloud as the opening prayer is unique to this retreat and meant to train our hearts to engage with the Psalms as they are meant to be read—as verbal, communal prayers to God. They encourage us to be honest about our pain, trusting that God walks with us in it.

Additional psalms of lament: 3–7; 10; 12–14; 17; 22; 25; 27–28; 30–31; 36; 39–44; 52–62; 64; 69–71; 73–74; 77; 79–80; 83; 85–86; 88–90; 94; 102; 120; 123; 126; 129; 139; and 141–142.

Supplies. In addition to a Bible and journal, bring paper (several colored sheets are ideal but anything will do) and an envelope. A candle is also highly encouraged on this retreat. The flame can represent the steady presence of Christ, the "light of the world" (Jn 8:12), with us in our loss.

⟫⟫⟩⟩ DAY ONE ⟨⟨⟨⟪

Begin by reviewing chapter five, the "Arrival Guide."

....

AFTERNOON

Bearing Our Burdens

OPENING SCRIPTURE—PSALM 34:18 NIV

The LORD is close to the brokenhearted and saves those who are crushed in spirit.

OPENING PRAYER

Light your candle, if you brought one, and read all of Psalm 42 aloud as your opening prayer.

REFLECTION

Grief often has a profound impact on the formation of our souls. Take gentle stock of where you are as you come into this retreat. It might be helpful to ask God, "What is the state of my soul?" Get out your journal and some paper, and try to take stock: What is the state or shape of your soul as you enter retreat?

Is it small, shrunken, and dehydrated, as the psalmist says, "My soul thirsts for . . . the living God" (Ps 42:2)? Is it downcast or disturbed (see Ps 42:5)? Maybe it is in turmoil: chaotic, scribbled lines moving in every direction (see Ps 42:11)? Or perhaps it feels round and robust: strong (see Ps 138:3)? Is it broken, fractured, all over the place (see Ps 34:18)?

Take a few moments to talk to God about this. When you are ready, draw the shape of your soul. If you brought Play-Doh or clay, you could use that to fashion a representation of your soul.

As you prepare to journey with your grief, keep in mind the gentle pace of Jesus. He was never harried nor hurried. He absorbed innumerable sorrows yet was never frantic and always kept pace with his Father.

WALKING WITH GRIEF

ANDY RAINE

Do not hurry
As you walk with grief;

It does not help the journey.

Walk slowly,
Pausing often:
Do not hurry
As you walk with grief.

Be not disturbed
By memories that come unbidden.
Swiftly forgive;
And let Christ speak for you
Unspoken words.
Unfinished conversation
Will be resolved in Him.
Be not disturbed.

Be gentle with the one
Who walks with grief.
If it is you,
Be gentle with yourself.
Swiftly forgive;
Walk slowly,
Pausing often.

Take time, be gentle
As you walk with grief.

As you hold this poem in your heart, take a slow stroll around your new landscape. Let your body lead the way, especially if you have been rushed and busy. Practice seeing the scenery, the people, and the natural beauty of your surroundings.

CLOSING PRAYER

Thank you, God, that you daily bear my burdens (see Ps 68:19 NIV), even when I do not see that it is you who sustains me. Help me keep pace with you as I walk with my grief; I receive your easy and light yoke that ties me to you. Help me to go where you go, pause when you pause, and rest when you rest. Amen.

....

EVENING

Blessed Are Those Who Mourn

OPENING SCRIPTURE—MATTHEW 5:3-4

Blessed are the poor in spirit, for theirs is the kingdom of heaven. Blessed are those who mourn, for they shall be comforted.

OPENING PRAYER

Light your candle, if you brought one, and read all of Psalm 44 aloud as your opening prayer.

REFLECTION

Read Matthew 5:1-11 several times slowly, imagining yourself in the scene.

Pay attention to what you hear, smell, or feel in this story. And pay attention to where you are in this story in proximity to Jesus and the rest of your community. These verses claim blessing over one who grieves. Consider how these words sound to you as you sit with your own grief. Look for places where you have received comfort, or places where you have not. Talk to the Lord about all that comes up in this time of imaginative prayer.

Richard Foster says, "By themselves the Spiritual Disciplines can do nothing; they can only get us to the place where something can be done. . . . [They are] the means by which we place ourselves where [God] can bless us." In *The Message* version of the Beatitudes we read, "You're blessed when you're at the end of your rope. With less of you there is more of God and his rule. You're blessed when you feel you've lost what is most dear to you. Only then can you be embraced by the One most dear to you" (Mt 5:3-4 MSG).

Questions for Journaling

- Who are you in the crowd in this Scripture passage?
- How close are you in proximity to Jesus? Do you want to be closer? Why or why not?
- How does it feel when he addresses you with these words, in light of your circumstances?
- Does any part of your grief feel like a blessing to you?
- What do you want to say to God about this?

CLOSING PRAYER

God, I confess I do not want to be poor in spirit; I do not want to mourn. These do not feel like places of blessing and providence. But I trust your Word, because you are a man familiar with sorrow. Please grant me wisdom, insight, love, understanding, and illumination to all that might need to be attended to on this retreat. Place a loving hedge of protection around me that I might not be overcome by my grief. Amen.

COMPLINE

Read the prayer for compline.

> Keep watch, dear Lord, with those who work, or watch, or weep this night, and give your angels charge over those who sleep. Tend the sick, Lord Christ; give rest to the weary, bless the dying, soothe the suffering, pity the afflicted, shield the joyous; and all for your love's sake. Amen. (Book of Common Prayer 1979)

Spend five minutes looking through your journal, reflecting on all you have experienced today.

End your evening with a prayer of examen:

What was life-giving to you today? Where did you feel the wind at your back?

What was draining for you today? What felt heavy or difficult?

Journal or otherwise explore these with God.

"The LORD is near to the brokenhearted and saves the crushed in spirit" (Ps 34:18). May Jesus be near you tonight, assuring you that the weight of your grief will not crush you. May the Lord bless you as you attend to your grief.

Gather together all the parts of yourself and present them to God. Receive this blessing:

> In peace I will lie down and fall asleep, for you alone, O Lord, make me dwell in safety. O come and bless the Lord, all you servants of the Lord, who stand by day and night in the house of the Lord. Lift up your hands to the holy place, and bless the Lord. May the all-powerful Lord grant us a restful night and a peaceful end. Amen.

﷽ DAY TWO ﷽

Rest upon waking. Have coffee in bed or follow any other practice that feels luxurious or comforting as you prepare to rest in Jesus today.

PRAYER OF RECOLLECTION

Move through these three phases of prayer each morning on your retreat, taking as long as you need for each one. Consider incorporating this prayer into your rhythm of life after returning home.

1. *Prayer of presentation.* Dear God, here I am. I present myself to you as one who is holy and pleasing to you. I lay out the pieces of my life before you, and let you see all that is within me. I acknowledge the unilateral nature of your love; all action starts with you. When I come to prayer, I am entering into a conversation I did not start and do not sustain. I wake to a day I did not create, into a universe I do not uphold, into a life I did not earn, and into circumstances I cannot control. Awaken my soul to the reality that I can do nothing apart from you. Thank you, that you are always with me and that I am never alone (see Rom 12:1-2; 8:34; Heb 1:3; Jn 15:5; Mt 28:20).

2. *Prayer of detachment.* Dear God, I let go of anything I try to gain apart from you. I am not defined by my roles: a good or bad mother or father, sister or brother, daughter or son, husband or wife, coworker, student, boss, or friend. These capacities do not define who I am, nor do health or sickness, poverty or wealth, success or

failure, applause or slander. I detach from these roles—
however vital and important; they are not at the core
of who I am. In places where I have managed to be
good, I count Christ more worthy than my success. In
areas where I have failed, I ask forgiveness and let go
of trying to make something of myself, proving myself
to the world, or trying to earn your love, which is given
freely (see Phil 3:7-8).

3. *Prayer of attachment.* Dear God, there is nothing you
would not do and have not done to make me your
own. I receive your mercy and grace. I was created
for union with you, and by Jesus' sacrifice, I am saved
from separation from you. At my center, I am in you
and you are in me. I can only locate my true self in
you. I am unrighteous on my own, but you are my
righteousness. I am chaotic on my own, but you have
given me the rightly ordered mind of Christ. Because
you have attached me to yourself and will never let me
go, I have full forgiveness, freedom, acceptance, and
pardon from my sin, guilt, and shame. I am blameless
in your sight. You delight in me and delight to co-
labor with me in the unique, good work you have
called me to. I am precious and irreplaceable to you.
No matter the circumstance in which I find myself,
I know that nothing comes to me that did not first
pass through the cross. No matter what else is true of
me in this life, at the center of my being is beloved
belonging; I am a child of God. There is nowhere I
can run where you will not follow, nowhere I can hide

where you will not find me. No matter how deep I go into my soul with you, I will find love, all the way down (see Col 1:22; Gal 2:20; Col 2:13-15; Rom 8:16; Ps 139:7-12).

Questions for Journaling

🖋 Which of these, if any, is difficult for your soul to receive?

🖋 Where are you feeling open to God today?

🖋 Which of these, if any, is hard for you to detach from?

🖋 What truths were you able to receive fully? Confess any unbelief.

MORNING

If You Had Been Here

OPENING SCRIPTURE—PSALM 10:1 NIV

Why, LORD, do you stand far off? Why do you hide yourself in times of trouble?

OPENING PRAYER

As you open in prayer this morning, consider if God feels "far off" or close by today. Talk with him about how you feel. Light your candle, if you brought one, and read all of Psalm 13 aloud as your opening prayer.

REFLECTION

Read John 11:1-37, placing yourself within the story. Imagine what it feels like to be in this scene, full of death, grief, and questioning. Maybe you are a bystander on the road or a family member. Maybe you are Mary or Martha. How does it feel to be present to this scene? What do you feel, see, hear, or touch?

Perhaps you find yourself as either Mary or Martha, who come to Jesus voicing the same concern. Place yourself in this moment, calling to mind a time when you wondered where God was.

Mary and Martha named their grief in this moment. They grieved the loss of their brother and also voiced their confusion over Jesus' lack of intervention—a second grief. They expressed what is often common in grief: wondering if Jesus can still be trusted, if he still was who they thought he was.

Questions for Journaling

- How does it feel for you to echo Mary and Martha's pleas? ("Where have you been?" "If you had been here, things might have been different!" "Why didn't you intervene?")
- How do you wish Jesus would have responded to them?
- How is Jesus responding to you?
- What questions does your grief have for Jesus?
- How does your grief want to be attended to in this extended time, when other things are not demanding your attention?
- Ask Jesus to be present with you as you attend to this part of you that has been neglected. What does it need now: A warm bath? A punching bag? A listening ear? To paint a picture or take a walk?

CLOSING PRAYER

Lord, there is much that I grieve and much that I do not understand, but I, too, believe that you are the resurrection and the life. Even if I cannot see the full picture now, I take you at your word. You are making all things new. Amen.

....

AFTERNOON

Pieces

OPENING SCRIPTURE—PSALM 38:9-10 NIV

All my longings lie open before you, Lord;
my sighing is not hidden from you.
My heart pounds, my strength fails me;
even the light has gone from my eyes.

OPENING PRAYER

Light your candle, if you brought one, and read all of Psalm 38 aloud as your opening prayer.

REFLECTION: PAPER EXERCISE

Sighing with the lungs, a pounding heart, muscle weakness for lack of strength, light gone from the eyes: all these are bodily responses to grief. Feeling shattered, broken, and fragmented is a natural response to grief. Coming apart is a scary emotion and is often very disorienting. What once was whole is now broken. We hear those experiencing grief say, "I've come undone," "A piece of me is missing," or "My heart is shattered."

Grief often comes to us in pieces, or as some describe it, waves. About a year after my mother-in-law died, I was cleaning out my son's closet. In the very back, wedged behind a forgotten box of dress shoes, was a specific toy car she had bought him for his first birthday. It didn't matter that this child was on the cusp of becoming a teenager; I remembered that moment as if it were yesterday. I remember thinking that among all the gifts I bought him, I never considered buying him a car because he was so young, and I didn't think it would appeal to him. But he loved it, and it quickly became his prized possession. I grew up with all girls, but she had birthed all boys. She knew instinctively what boys would like.

I found myself slumped in his closet, choking back tears. I had processed so many aspects of grief for my mother-in-law that this surprised me. I grieved her as a lost friend, mentor, even grandma for my kids. But this specific piece felt fresh and raw: I grieved losing someone in my corner who instinctively knew boys. She had three and I had three. And she would not be here to mentor me through the distinct challenges of raising boys. I would have to do it without her. I had to name this specific aspect of my grief, as it was distinct from all others and deserved its own place in my broken heart.

Take out the colored paper you brought, tear it into pieces, and write on each a specific facet of your grief. Try to name as many as possible. We wither spiritually when we fail to name things properly, since naming our grief accurately gives it the dignity it deserves. (Some examples of what you might write on your pieces: "Laughter: this piece represents the laughter I shared with my friend. No one made me laugh

like her, and I'm afraid I might never laugh the same again."
Or, "Safe: This piece represents how cared for my loved one
made me feel. I felt safe, and now that safety is gone.")

After you have given language to as many pieces of
your grief as possible, put them in the envelope. On the
outside of the envelope write "God" or all of Colossians
1:17, "And [Jesus] is before all things, and in him all things
hold together." This envelope symbolizes God holding all
your pieces. He will put them back together—most likely
in his own formation and timing. Still, he can be trusted
with them.

"It is better to come to God with sharp words than to
remain distant from him, never voicing our doubts and dis-
appointments. Better to rage at the Creator than to smolder
in polite devotion. God did not smite the psalmist. Through
the Psalms, he dares us to speak to him bluntly."

Questions for Journaling

- How do you feel after completing this exercise?
- How might you continue to attend to your bodily responses to grief?
- How can you let your body lead the way?
- What sharp words does your grief want to express to God right now?

CLOSING PRAYER

"I lay out the pieces of my life on the altar and wait for your
fire to fall upon my heart" (Ps 5:3 TPT). God, you alone
hold my life in your hands, every fractured piece. I trust that
I am held together by you. Amen.

EVENING

A Man of Sorrows

OPENING SCRIPTURE—ISAIAH 53:3-4

[Jesus] was despised and rejected by men,
a man of sorrows and acquainted with grief;
and as one from whom men hide their faces
he was despised, and we esteemed him not.

Surely he has borne our griefs
and carried our sorrows;
yet we esteemed him stricken,
smitten by God, and afflicted.

OPENING PRAYER

Read all of Psalm 22 aloud as your opening prayer.

REFLECTION

Read Psalm 22 in its entirety as many times as you like to familiarize yourself with it. Now rewrite parts or all of this Psalm in your own language, using the grief events from your own life as your guide.

Questions for Journaling

- What parts of the psalm resonate most to you?
- What surprises you?
- What connections are you making between your own grief and the person of Jesus as a "man of sorrows"?
- What is it like to pray this prayer to God knowing he inclines his ear to what you are saying to him (see Ps 102:2), that he is interested in this prayer and receives it?

Close this time of prayer with what is often called the Jesus Prayer, based on Luke 18:38. Use this as a centering prayer exercise, praying it slowly and repeatedly to ground yourself in the reality of God's presence with you.

Jesus Christ,

Son of God

Have mercy on me, a sinner.

COMPLINE

Read the prayer for compline.

Keep watch, dear Lord, with those who work, or watch, or weep this night, and give your angels charge over those who sleep. Tend the sick, Lord Christ; give rest to the weary, bless the dying, soothe the suffering, pity the afflicted, shield the joyous; and all for your love's sake. Amen. (Book of Common Prayer 1979)

Spend five minutes looking through your journal, reflecting on all you have experienced today.

Pick a few stanzas from the psalm you wrote in your own heart's language, and consider this as you enter a prayer of examen:

What was life-giving to you today? Where did you feel the wind at your back?

What was draining for you today? What felt heavy or difficult?

Journal or otherwise explore these with God.

"The LORD is near to the brokenhearted and saves the crushed in spirit" (Ps 34:18). May Jesus be near you tonight, assuring you that the weight of your grief will not crush you.

May the Lord bless you as you attend to your grief.

Gather together all the parts of yourself and present them to God. Receive this blessing:

> In peace I will lie down and fall asleep, for you alone, O Lord, make me dwell in safety. O come and bless the Lord, all you servants of the Lord, who stand by day and night in the house of the Lord. Lift up your hands to the holy place, and bless the Lord. May the all-powerful Lord grant us a restful night and a peaceful end. Amen.

⟩⟩⟩⟩ DAY THREE ⟨⟨⟨⟨

Rest upon waking. Have coffee in bed or follow any other practice that feels luxurious or comforting as you prepare to rest in Jesus today.

PRAYER OF RECOLLECTION
Refer to day two.

....

MORNING

But God

OPENING SCRIPTURE—PSALM 102:1-2

Hear my prayer, O LORD;
let my cry come to you!
Do not hide your face from me
in the day of my distress!
Incline your ear to me;
answer me speedily in the day when I call!

OPENING PRAYER

Read all of Psalm 73 aloud as your opening prayer.

REFLECTION

Now that you've sat with different facets of your grief for an extended period, take some time to explore what most stands out to you. At the beginning of our retreat we drew a picture of the soul; now we are giving it more space, more like a map than a single picture. Take a moment and draw a map of your soul. There might be parts of your soul that feel healthy and thriving, and others that are broken and in need of healing. Try to pay attention to these differences. See if you have named griefs you have not recognized before. See if any parts of your grief feel stuck or lodged somewhere in your body. Pay attention to any parts of this soul map that still feel closed or inaccessible to you.

Gerald Sittser said, "What is true of the body is also true of the soul. The pain of loss is severe because the pleasure of life is so great; it demonstrates the supreme value of what is lost." He also wrote, "Loss can also make us more. In the darkness we can still find the light. In death we can also find life."

Many of the lament psalms include a contrast of thought often signaled by the word *but*. You just read one in Psalm 73:26: "My flesh and my heart may fail, but God is the strength of my heart and my portion forever." The lament psalms often follow a familiar pattern: The psalmist pours out their heart to the Lord and then contrasts that with what they remember about God in the face of their sorrows. Nearly every lament psalm includes an element like this. Take a moment to articulate your own "but God"—your own assertion of God's providence and power available to you even in the face of grief.

Questions for Journaling

- What is your "but God" that you will take home from this retreat? Can you locate it on your soul map?
- Where can you see light or life where you did not before?
- Where has your soul expanded in grief?
- What glimpses of abundance can you praise God for?
- What response do you want to offer that represents your "but God" moment?

CLOSING PRAYER

Thank you, God, that you are the container that holds all my grief, since it is too big and heavy for me; you are able to hold all things together (see Col 1:17). Thank you that you alone are familiar with all the different places in my soul and that you bear all my burdens. Thank you, God, that you have dealt bountifully with me on this retreat. Place your Holy Spirit as a seal over this time of healing. Amen.

>>><§<><<

As you pack up, do so mindfully, keeping your slow pace as you walk with grief.

A BLESSING AS YOU GO

JAMES BRYAN SMITH

You are one in whom Christ dwells and delights;
You live in the unshakable kingdom of God.
The kingdom of God is not in trouble,
And neither are you.
Go in peace.

FOR ONE IN NEED OF DISCERNMENT

✝

Often when we think of discernment, we think about a choice that must be made. We might need to discern the next right thing: a move, a career change, or a relationship choice. These decisions often boil down to options A versus B, a choice best decided on by a list of pros and cons. Should I marry this person? Should I take this or that job? Many questions of discernment illuminate questions of vocation: What am I meant to do? Who am I meant to be?

It's not inherently wrong for decision-making to mark the starting point for our conversation. I assume most are drawn to this retreat for this reason. But know in advance, this is where we begin, not where we end. God surely cares about the season you are in and is faithful to guide you "along the best pathway for your life" (Ps 32:8 NLT), yet God more often guides us into new territories of our soul than to locations on a map.

On this retreat we will unpack some deeper movements of discernment that require us to tune in to our longings and see what they might show us about our relationship with God. We will pay attention to our vices, such as envy, that may turn us to shame when it's meant to turn us to God. And we will get closer to the root of that gooey middle place between God's action in our lives and our own.

It will be helpful for us to pay attention to Jesus' first disciples who had careers, vocations, aspirations, and obligations before Jesus came along. In the Gospels, Jesus was often recorded saying only two words, "Follow me" (Mt 4:19; 16:24), and those from fishermen to politicians ceased their work and did as he said. Sometimes life is like this: God intervenes directly—closes the door, blocks the path, presents an invitation—and we are faced with continuing to follow him or going our own way. Yet even when the career, relationship, or path remains unclear, the command is always the same: "Follow me."

What I like best about the disciples is the flimsiness of their faith. It gives me hope for mine. They slept and ate and camped with Jesus day after day for years. They heard him promise all the great things he would do through all the unique callings he had placed on their lives. Yet when Jesus was captured, crucified, and raised from the dead—all events he foretold to them—they did not know what to do, so they went back to their boring old jobs.

We find the disciples James and John mending nets when Jesus first calls them (see Mt 4:21; Mk 1:19), and after Jesus' resurrection, we find Peter back in this same location fishing (see Jn 21:3). It's worth paying attention when the Gospel writers tuck seemingly useless information into their narratives. Why does it matter if they were mending nets?

Why not assume they were picking dirt out of their nails or staring off into space? It turns out the phrase "mending nets"—a term meant to focus us on the disciples' vocation—is rich with theological meaning. Paul borrows the same Greek word, *kataritzō* (mending nets) to talk about the work of a Christian. Our vocation is to mend, prepare, and restore (Gal 6:1, Eph 4:12, 1 Thess 3:10) while God prepares and equips us for the good work he has given us to do (Heb 13:20-21; 1 Pet 5:10). We are the vessels though which God is mending the world back to himself.

This verb, *to mend*, "indicates the close relationship between character and destiny." The character of a thing, what it is made of, reflects its ultimate destiny. The nets—made of fiber and twine or whatever nets are made of—reflect what the net is made *for*: catching fish. The same is true for us. We tend to become hyperfocused on what we are made to *do*. This can be true even in the church, where whole classes exist to assess one's spiritual gifts. They ask, What am I made for? What am I good at? How does God want to use me? These questions are not wrong, just out of order. God does not primarily want to use you; God primarily wants to love you.

We want to know what we are made *for*, but often God shows us what we are made *of*, and the two are intricately connected. We are woven and spun in the depths of the earth (see Ps 139:15), made in the image of God himself (see Gen 1:27), and God continues to re-form our souls into the image of his Son, Jesus (see Rom 8:29). This is his plan and his gift. We are mended and tended daily into what we ought to be. Resting assured in what we are made of can show us the relationship between our character and our destiny. We are being made fit for eternity with him. We are made of and for love.

In his book *Courage and Calling*, Gordon Smith offers a framework of three "expressions of vocation":

The general call—the invitation to follow Jesus; to be Christian

The specific call—a vocation that is unique to a person; that individual's mission in the world

The immediate responsibilities—those tasks or duties that God calls us to today

When thinking about discernment, we often focus on the specific call to the detriment of the other two. These three aspects, although distinct, remain fluid. Examining our immediate responsibilities, say changing a diaper or paying the bills, may offer greater insight into the specific call of being a mother or running a home or business. The general call gives weight to all others, since everything we do is for the glory of God.

We must consider how our daily rhythms, our immediate responsibilities, form us into a particular kind of person. Big vocational decisions are not the only location for choice. True discernment begins with the small, daily habits that make up our lives, where we learn to love what God loves, choosing easily and instinctively what Jesus might choose in any given situation.

⊱⊰⊱⊰ DAY ONE ⊱⊰⊱⊰

Begin by reviewing chapter five, the "Arrival Guide."

....

AFTERNOON

A Quiet Life

OPENING SCRIPTURE—1 THESSALONIANS 4:11-12 NIV

Make it your ambition to lead a quiet life: You should mind your own business and work with your hands, just as we told you, so that your daily life may win the respect of outsiders and so that you will not be dependent on anybody.

OPENING PRAYER

God, you are light, and in you there is no darkness at all.

Let the light of Christ shine into all the dark corners of my heart. Amen.

REFLECTION

Ask God what about your daily life he finds faithful and pleasing to him. List everything that comes to mind. Rest for a few moments in the gaze of God who "sees in secret" and rewards in secret (Mt 6:6).

In *Courage and Calling*, Gordon T. Smith says, "The quality of our work depends, in large measure, on the integrity of the work we do when others are not watching. This is true of all work; all vocations. . . . We either learn to work in obscurity or we do not learn how to work at all."

Sit for a few moments and assess any places where you feel resistance to the quiet, daily, hidden practices God has called you to.

Smith then calls on the imagery of the Proverbs 31 woman to help us make sense of our work/life balance (managing a home and having a career). This balance is required of both men and women, parents and non-parents. We are all called to care for the body God has given us and all its needs for food, clean clothes, meaningful activity, and restful spaces. Smith says, "The woman of Proverbs 31 is clearly engaged on both fronts. And by implication it is important to observe that there is no inherent tension between them. Indeed, perhaps the two are essential to each other, authenticating or legitimizing the other."

Questions for Journaling

- Look over the list you made, and ask God to attribute meaning to these aspects in your life.
- Where have you overlooked things that God values?
- What does it feel like to let God be proud of you in these ways?
- Where do you feel a tension in your work/life balance?
- What do you wish you could change?
- Proverbs 31:18 in *The Message* reads, "She senses the worth of her work." Sit with God for a moment and ask honestly if you sense the worth of the work he has entrusted to you. Where is this easy? Where is this hard?

CLOSING PRAYER

End this time of prayer by thanking God for all the hidden, mundane, overlooked places in your life where he loves you and calls you to co-labor alongside him.

EVENING

Envy and Exhaustion

OPENING SCRIPTURE—GENESIS 25:27-33

Esau was a skillful hunter, a man of the field, while Jacob was a quiet man, dwelling in tents. . . . Once when Jacob was cooking stew, Esau came in from the field, and he was exhausted. And Esau said to Jacob, "Let me eat some of that red stew, for I am exhausted!" . . . Jacob said, "Sell me your birthright now." . . . So he . . . sold his birthright to Jacob.

OPENING PRAYER

Dear God, on my own I am chaotic, but you give me the rightly ordered mind of Christ (see 1 Cor 2:16). You do not give me "a spirit of fear, but of power and of love and of a sound mind" (2 Tim 1:7 NKJV). I receive that now, as I am aware that I am all over the place, my heart drawn in so many directions to so many things. Help me to will and to want only you. Amen.

REFLECTION

In this Scripture, we find twins Jacob and Esau battling with envy and exhaustion. Esau has come in from the fields exhausted, depleted, and in prime condition to make the terrible, life-altering decision of giving up his birthright. Jacob capitalizes on Esau's weakened state, his envy driving him to steal his brother's blessing and inheritance.

Most Christians reject envy—the desire for what belongs to another—and rightly so. But envy has a hidden gem in its center: it shows us what we long for. Envy, while an unproductive place to dwell in the long term, can offer a guidepost along the road, pointing us toward deeper, perhaps hidden desires.

We may envy someone's career, family, home, or life stage. Take a moment for one of these examples to float to the surface. Call to mind someone in your life who you find yourself envying. Ask God to illuminate key characteristics about how your own perceived deficiency intersects with this desire. Sit for a moment with the Lord, and let him show you what he wants you to see in this. Sometimes envy is sparked by dissatisfaction in our own vocation. This can be a helpful indicator that a change is needed. Smith says, "Everyone is invited to do good work that they are not craving to avoid."

Questions for Journaling

- What aspects of your work (paid or unpaid) do you find yourself "craving to avoid"?
- What aspects do you envy in someone else's work?
- What connections are you making between envy and any exhaustion you might be feeling?
- When do you feel most tired or bored during your day?
- Where does your soul gravitate to in boredom? What do you find yourself doing?
- As you more deeply engage with this retreat, what work do you notice you are relieved to leave behind? (This can include emotional labor along with relational situations you are pleased to be removed from.) Take a moment to see how you might want to physically release anything you are still carrying with you. What could symbolize

letting it go? What could be an external representation
of this internal reality? Use the rest of your evening to
do this.

CLOSING PRAYER

Thank you, God, that you have given me good work to do
that you have not given to another. Help me be content to
work and rest beside you. Amen.

COMPLINE

Read the prayer for compline.

Keep watch, dear Lord, with those who work, or watch,
or weep this night, and give your angels charge over
those who sleep. Tend the sick, Lord Christ; give rest to
the weary, bless the dying, soothe the suffering, pity the
afflicted, shield the joyous; and all for your love's sake.
Amen. (Book of Common Prayer 1979)

Spend five minutes looking through your journal, reflecting on all you have experienced today.

End your evening with a prayer of examen:

What was life-giving to you today? Where did you feel
the wind at your back?

What was draining for you today? What felt heavy or
difficult?

Journal or otherwise explore these with God.

꙳꙳꙳꙳❁꙳꙳꙳꙳

Gather together all the parts of yourself and present them
to God. Receive this blessing:

In peace I will lie down and fall asleep, for you alone, O Lord, make me dwell in safety. O come and bless the Lord, all you servants of the Lord, who stand by day and night in the house of the Lord. Lift up your hands to the holy place, and bless the Lord. May the all-powerful Lord grant us a restful night and a peaceful end. Amen.

⟩⟩⟩⟩ DAY TWO ⟨⟨⟨⟨

Rest upon waking. Have coffee in bed or follow any other practice that feels luxurious or comforting as you prepare to rest in Jesus today.

PRAYER OF RECOLLECTION

Move through these three phases of prayer each morning on your retreat, taking as long as you need for each one. Consider incorporating this prayer into your rhythm of life after returning home.

1. ***Prayer of presentation.*** Dear God, here I am. I present myself to you as one who is holy and pleasing to you. I lay out the pieces of my life before you, and let you see all that is within me. I acknowledge the unilateral nature of your love; all action starts with you. When I come to prayer, I am entering into a conversation I did not start and do not sustain. I wake to a day I did not create, into a universe I do not uphold, into a life I did not earn, and into circumstances I cannot control. Awaken my soul to the reality that I can do nothing apart from you. Thank you, that you are always with me and that I am never alone (see Rom 12:1-2; 8:34; Heb 1:3; Jn 15:5; Mt 28:20).

2. *Prayer of detachment.* Dear God, I let go of anything I try to gain apart from you. I am not defined by my roles: a good or bad mother or father, sister or brother, daughter or son, husband or wife, coworker, student, boss, or friend. These capacities do not define who I am, nor do health or sickness, poverty or wealth, success or failure, applause or slander. I detach from these roles—however vital and important; they are not at the core of who I am. In places where I have managed to be good, I count Christ more worthy than my success. In areas where I have failed, I ask forgiveness and let go of trying to make something of myself, proving myself to the world, or trying to earn your love, which is given freely (see Phil 3:7-8).

3. *Prayer of attachment.* Dear God, there is nothing you would not do and have not done to make me your own. I receive your mercy and grace. I was created for union with you, and by Jesus' sacrifice, I am saved from separation from you. At my center, I am in you and you are in me. I can only locate my true self in you. I am unrighteous on my own, but you are my righteousness. I am chaotic on my own, but you have given me the rightly ordered mind of Christ. Because you have attached me to yourself and will never let me go, I have full forgiveness, freedom, acceptance, and pardon from my sin, guilt, and shame. I am blameless in your sight. You delight in me and delight to co-labor with me in the unique, good work you have called me to. I am precious and irreplaceable to you. No matter the circumstance in which I find myself, I know that nothing

comes to me that did not first pass through the cross. No matter what else is true of me in this life, at the center of my being is beloved belonging; I am a child of God. There is nowhere I can run where you will not follow, nowhere I can hide where you will not find me. No matter how deep I go into my soul with you, I will find love, all the way down (see Col 1:22; Gal 2:20; Col 2:13-15; Rom 8:16; Ps 139:7-12).

Questions for Journaling

🖉 Which of these, if any, is difficult for your soul to receive?

🖉 Where are you feeling open to God today?

🖉 Which of these, if any, is hard for you to detach from?

🖉 What truths were you able to receive fully? Confess any unbelief.

MORNING

Content

OPENING SCRIPTURE—JOHN 10:3

The sheep hear his voice, and he calls his own sheep by name and leads them out.

OPENING PRAYER

Jesus, you were never harried nor frantic. Faced with endless demands, repetitive needs, and the tugging and pulling of the crowd, still you walked gently on the earth. Let me walk gently into today. Let me keep pace with you. Give me courage, and let me learn from you. Amen.

REFLECTION

For each of today's sections of prayer, we will focus on three key elements of discernment that help us hear God speak. This is not a topic that can be fully covered in this space, yet we will briefly consider how God chooses to speak to his people via *content*, *context*, and *cadence*.

This morning we will look first at *content*: What does God say? An easy example is Scripture, the breathed-out Word of God meant to teach, correct, and guide his people (see 2 Tim 3:16). Daily time immersed in the Scriptures is invaluable for anyone seeking to hear from God. I've heard it said that we cannot keep our Bibles closed and wonder why we never hear from God. But we often reduce the Scriptures to an ancient manuscript instead of the living sword it is meant to be: enlivened through the Holy Spirit, able to slash through our defenses and reveal what is hidden in our hearts (see Heb 4:12). The Holy Spirit is called our counselor, able to guide us into all truth (see Jn 16:13), addressing us directly through God's Word—not a dusty, dead, irrelevant book but the living Word of God.

Through the Scriptures, God calls us to a host of many good things: caring for the poor, loving our neighbor, serving the least, and turning the other cheek, to name a few. Without the Scriptures, we lose sight of the heart of God. But without the Holy Spirit we cannot fully discern what we are called to today. Part of examining the content of what God says is considering what God might have for us here and now, with these specific people, in this space and time.

To let the content of God's Word dwell richly within us, we will read Hebrews 4:9-12. Read this Scripture lectio divina style, reading it several times and pausing between to let God speak in whatever way he wishes. This is not a time for study, but a time to be refreshed and nourished by the living Word of God given to you. (Review the four movements of lectio divina in chapter two.)

> There remains a Sabbath rest for the people of God, for whoever has entered God's rest has also rested from his works as God did from his.
>
> Let us therefore strive to enter that rest, so that no one may fall by the same sort of disobedience. For the word of God is living and active, sharper than any two-edged sword, piercing to the division of soul and of spirit, of joints and of marrow, and discerning the thoughts and intentions of the heart. (Hebrews 4:9-12)

In the second reading, reflect on a word or phrase that shimmered or stood out to you. Give yourself a few minutes to do this. Then ask God, "How does this connect with my life today? What do I need to know or be or do?"

In the third reading, prepare yourself to respond to God.

Questions for Journaling

- How might entering rest protect us from disobedience?
- Have you ever considered rest as an act of obedience?
- What connections are you making between striving "to enter that rest" of God and the nature of God's Word as discerning the "intentions of the heart"?
- What thoughts, intentions, or motivations of your heart is God revealing in this time? What do you want to tell him?

In the fourth reading, simply rest. Do as you are led. Is God asking you to wait on him, hand something over, or rest more deeply in him? Sit in the loving presence of God—the One who beckons you to come away with him.

CLOSING PRAYER

Thank you, God, that "The heavens declare the glory of God, and the sky above proclaims his handiwork. Day to day pours out speech, and night to night reveals knowledge" (Ps 19:1-2). Amen.

As you continue your prayerful posture, go outside and spend twenty minutes with Psalm 19 simply listening, looking for, and attending to what God is saying through his creation. Pay attention to what you see, smell, hear, feel, and receive through your senses. Gather an object or take a picture of something that stood out to you from this time.

....

AFTERNOON

Context

OPENING SCRIPTURE—JOHN 10:4

When he has brought out all his own, he goes before them, and the sheep follow him, for they know his voice.

OPENING PRAYER

Dear God,
Give me eyes to see,
Ears to hear
and a heart to know you more. Amen.

REFLECTION

We converse with God, both hearing and speaking, in the *context* of our broader relationship with him. Dallas Willard says we must consider "the kind of relationship God intends to have with his people. If we give primacy to forms of communication that God does not in the whole prefer in relation to his children, that will hinder our understanding of and cooperation with his voice." Here Willard points out the human propensity to turn to God when we need a divine revelation, a flash of insight, or a burst of emotion to meet a need. But God prefers to journey with his children, talking with them on the intimate path through details of everyday life. God occasionally acts in supernatural ways, intervening in human lives with signs and wonders, but more often his work is slow and steady, walked out over the course of a lifetime. Our motives are often good; we think if God would just intervene directly, it would leave little room for error or misunderstanding on our part. But when we trade the lifelong work of discernment for a quick fix we miss how God prefers to communicate with us—as beloved children with whom he desires an ongoing, ever-deepening, daily, familiar, intimate conversation.

Hearing the particulars of what God wants us to do is only one part of our ongoing communication with God, and arguably not even the most important. I hold my children close and tell them how much I love them before sending them off to school in the morning, and I hope they retain those words in their hearts more than the sentence before, when I told them to make their beds and brush their teeth. One sentence contained good habits to instill a healthy and ordered life, but the other is vital to how I want them to see themselves in the context of our relationship and their purpose in the world. We must consider that God addresses us not as slaves but as his children who walk in love (Gal 4:7). We are invited to know his heart and intentions, which matter just as much as the content of his orders. God wants to dine with us, rest with us, tarry with us, and enjoy our voice and presence as much as we enjoy his.

Read John 10:1-4. Imagine yourself in this scene and Jesus addressing you directly.

Questions for Journaling

- What do you feel as you hear these words?
- When have you preferred your style of communication over God's?
- What are some ways you are currently seeking answers or a sense of peace for a decision you must make?
- Where have you been resistant to Jesus' leading?
- What does Jesus want to say to you about this?

CLOSING PRAYER

End your time of prayer by acknowledging places in your life where you have preferred quick answers rather than God's presence. Rest for a few moments with the One who will never leave you nor forsake you (see Deut 31:6).

EVENING

Cadence

OPENING SCRIPTURE—JOHN 10:5, 27

A stranger they will not follow, but they will flee from him, for they do not know the voice of strangers. . . . My sheep hear my voice, and I know them, and they follow me.

OPENING PRAYER

God, you have made your voice known to me through your word, through creation, through other people, and through the circumstances of my life. I want to know your voice even more and attend to it all the days of my life. Be merciful to me in this time of discernment. Open my ears to your word to me today and soften my heart to receive it. Amen.

REFLECTION

We will begin this evening session with a freewriting exercise on the topic: How does God's voice sound to you?

As we turn now to *cadence*, take a few moments and ask God to reveal the last time he addressed you directly. This can be last week or the last decade, and most likely is a time only discernible with the benefit of hindsight. Take some time to get clear on the situation: what happened, who was involved, what questions or conflicts arose. Now journal for about five to ten minutes on the details of what happened and how you came to discern God's voice in that situation. Most particularly, What did God's voice sound like? How did you feel when you heard it? Write about the experience until you have a few solid adjectives describing what God's voice sounded like to you.

Many people, when led through this exercise, return with similar themes: The voice of God was gentle, kind, playful, full of peace, warm, or comforting. This is the *cadence* of God's voice, how it sounds to you, not simply the black-and-white text, verse, or words that were spoken. God often calls his people to new, surprising, countercultural activities. We might not always know *what* God calls us to specifically, so it benefits us to remember *how* he speaks to us as well. Marjorie Thompson says, "It seems significant that the Bible likens us to sheep, not cattle. In Scripture, sheep are not driven but led."

Compare this posture of God being in front of us, guiding our path, to other voices that you feel might be driving you from behind. These barking voices of the world often tell us to do more, aim higher, go faster, be better. What are some of these for you? (Some examples: "I have to," "I should," "I need to.")

Questions for Journaling

- Make two columns. On one side put what adjectives you used to describe God's voice: warm, playful, kind, etc. On the other side, write how it feels to be driven on by your own or the world's standards: anxious, nervous, hurried, etc.
- Where do these voices on the second side come from? The internalized voices of your caregivers, the enemy, the surrounding culture, or your own beliefs about yourself?
- How do these alternative voices contrast with the voice of the Good Shepherd? Ask God if there are any voices you need to reject outright as false indicators of discernment.

✐ John 10:4 reads, "When he has brought out all his own, he goes before them." How has God gone before you in life's circumstances? How has he made a way? How has he led you gently and confidently?

CLOSING PRAYER

End this time by prayerfully rereading the verses from John 10, asking God to help you discern and respond to his voice. Close your time of prayer with a bow of reverence to God, or simply place your hand to your chest, feeling your own heartbeat, as a gesture acknowledging God's care for you and presence with you.

><><><❁><><><

Rest, eat a nutritious dinner, and maybe take a slow stroll. Practice being in your own body, if you have been rushed and busy. Practice seeing the scenery, the people, and the natural beauty of your surroundings.

COMPLINE

Read the prayer for compline.

Keep watch, dear Lord, with those who work, or watch, or weep this night, and give your angels charge over those who sleep. Tend the sick, Lord Christ; give rest to the weary, bless the dying, soothe the suffering, pity the afflicted, shield the joyous; and all for your love's sake. Amen. (Book of Common Prayer 1979)

Spend five minutes looking through your journal, reflecting on all you have experienced today.

End your evening with a prayer of examen:

What was life-giving to you today? Where did you feel the wind at your back?

What was draining for you today? What felt heavy or difficult?

Journal or otherwise explore these with God.

❊

Gather together all the parts of yourself and present them to God. Receive this blessing:

> In peace I will lie down and fall asleep, for you alone, O Lord, make me dwell in safety. O come and bless the Lord, all you servants of the Lord, who stand by day and night in the house of the Lord. Lift up your hands to the holy place, and bless the Lord. May the all-powerful Lord grant us a restful night and a peaceful end. Amen.

DAY THREE

Rest upon waking. Have coffee in bed or follow any other practice that feels luxurious or comforting as you prepare to rest in Jesus today.

PRAYER OF RECOLLECTION

Refer to day two.

....

MORNING

Adult Children

OPENING SCRIPTURE—2 TIMOTHY 1:12

For I know whom I have believed, and I am convinced that he is able to guard until that day what has been entrusted to me.

OPENING PRAYER

Spend a few moments as you open in prayer, asking God to reveal all that he has entrusted to you. Some scriptural examples: We are entrusted with the gospel (see 1 Thess 2:4), entrusted with the message of reconciliation (see 2 Cor 5:19), entrusted with our calling, our purpose, and even life itself (see 2 Tim 1:8-12).

>}}}}}⚜}}}}{

God, you have put much into my care and many people in my sphere of influence. Give me eyes to see all that has been entrusted to me and show me how to steward these gifts for the sake of your kingdom. Amen.

REFLECTION

Yesterday we touched on a concept important to our interactions with God and our ability to discern his voice. We are God's children, no longer slaves,

> *In many cases our need to wonder about or be told what God wants in a certain situation is a clear indication of how little we are engaged in his work.*
>
> DALLAS WILLARD

called into an interactive parent-child relationship with him. But, while we are children, we are not meant to remain helpless infants tossed about by the circumstances of life (see Eph 4:13-14).

We are called to be God's children, adult children, who subsist on solid food (see Heb 5:12-14). Infants cannot be trained in discernment. Adults have agency, the capacity to no longer conform to the patterns of this world but be transformed by the renewal of their minds, that "by testing you may discern what is the will of God" (Rom 12:2). Adult children are equipped to discern and make choices as they co-labor with God to advance his kingdom on the earth (see 1 Cor 3:9). In other words, God will not often intervene to make your choices for you but instead equips you by the power of the Holy Spirit to become a good chooser.

Questions for Journaling

- Does the idea of how much God has entrusted to you scare or excite you?
- How does it feel that God wants to help you become a good chooser?
- In what situations have you abdicated responsibility for fear of making a mistake? When have you been afraid to choose?
- What did you bring into this retreat with you?
- What are you leaving behind? Release all of these to the Lord and affirm who you are in him—beloved, free, delightful, celebrated adult child, and heir.
- What will you carry with you out of this retreat?

CLOSING PRAYER

Try to leave the last thirty minutes to an hour of your retreat to sit in silent prayer, perhaps with the image or object from creation (day two). Entrust yourself to the God who trusts you, who knows you, cares for you, and loves you beyond measure.

As you transition into leaving your retreat, even as you pack up your belongings, leave room to do it slowly, mindfully, and in step with the Holy Spirit.

A BLESSING AS YOU GO

CARDINAL NEWMAN

God has created me
to do Him some definite service.
He has committed some work to me
which He has not committed to another.
I have my mission—
I may never know what it in this life.
But I shall be told it in the next. . . .
I am a link in a chain,
a bond of connection between persons.
He has not created me for naught.
I shall do good, I shall do His work. . . .
Therefore, I will trust Him.
Whatever, wherever I am,
I cannot be thrown away . . .
He does nothing in vain.
He knows what He is about.

Part Three

✝

RETURNING

11

REENTRY

†

My first forty-eight-hour retreat was a disaster. Halfway up the mountain my phone lost its signal, so I could not contact the owner to ask if I was meant to stay at the main house or one of the smaller dwellings. I was left reading and re-reading the terse instructions I jotted down beforehand. I settled into the main house and, aware of my exhaustion, crawled into bed in the main bedroom and promptly fell asleep. I was awakened forty-five minutes later by a sharp knocking at the front door. I leaped out of bed, rumpled and disoriented, and opened the door to find two men staring quizzically at me. They were the host and the retreatant who was meant to stay in the main house. I apologized profusely then excused myself to make the bed and tidy the space I had already begun to sprawl throughout. The small cabin next door that was mine was cozy and inviting, but I felt unsettled by my mistake.

I was awed by the space and the weather. The first day was unseasonably warm for November in the mountains, like summer was heaving its final exhale before extinguishing

for the season. The next day, Saturday, was a cool and crisp autumn day, orange leaves against a cerulean sky. By three a.m. the next morning, the weather turned dramatically, and I woke up Sunday morning to a curtain of snow falling so fast an inch or two already began to stick to the ground. I took my time packing up, enjoying the falling snow, feeling grateful for experiencing so many seasons in one weekend. I stayed so long that by the time I tried to leave, I slid across the driveway, unable to get a foothold on the ice hidden beneath the snow. I realized I would have to take all my belongings in one trip, since once I made it down the hill to my car, I would not be able to climb back up. The gratitude slipped away from me, degree by degree, as I slid ungracefully down the hill to my car, dragging all my belongings with me. I loaded myself in, and with soaking pants, began to ease my car down the mountain. I got less than a mile on the snowy ice before I slid into a ditch. I had to call AAA and get towed down the mountain.

The foibles and mishaps during my retreat were perhaps a welcome distraction from what was happening to me internally. I had attended large group conferences. I had attended smaller, intimate retreats with others. I had enjoyed day retreats with my nun friends. I even scheduled secluded weekends away dedicated to writing. But this was my first extended time alone with God holding no alternative agenda. I had a lot brewing under the surface of my soul, and I pictured engaging with God in one of two ways: either wrestling it out, like Jacob and his hip, or God downloading a torrent of holy insight for me to catch, something akin to Moses receiving the Ten Commandments. What I was not at all prepared for was silence.

I remember going on a walk that first evening through the woods, the silence so strong it felt oppressive. I could only hear the crunch of my shoes on dried twigs, and when I paused, my ears ached with the vastness and the pulse of my own heartbeat. I prayed:

God, I'm ready. I have arranged all the childcare. I have made all the food. I am all yours. Give me what you have for me. If you want to free me from what enslaves me, I'm ready. Reveal it! Let's go! If you want to downpour your Spirit, I have a pen. I'm ready to take notes!

I opened my hands and my heart, the extensive valley beneath me, purple mountains as far as I could see. Beautiful, echoing silence. Nothing.

The longer God went without speaking, the more despondent I became. I prepared really beautiful and delicious food for my trip and enjoyed every meal. I was aware of a deep level of exhaustion, so I let myself nap when needed. I took long walks; I put on the fire; I made myself one million cups of tea as the weather turned overnight from fall to winter. I had the whole recipe for a perfect retreat. Why was God silent? Why was he not participating?

My frustration with God boiled over as I was being towed down the mountain: *What was the point of this? I'm never doing this again.* I got home late that night, hungry and exhausted, disappointed and disillusioned. My husband expected me to come home in a Zen-like state of bliss, so when he saw my face he asked, "What's the matter?"

"Nothing," I mumbled, hauling up my suitcase and brushing past him.

He persisted. "I thought you would come back relaxed."

In his words I heard an unmet expectation that mirrored and layered on my own, becoming a burden too heavy to bear, breaking something within me. I started yelling at him, how he didn't understand or support me, how he was never there for me. I watched myself pick a fight with the wrong person. A small voice within me said, "These are the words you need to say to God."

I apologized, excused myself, and locked myself in our bedroom. I cried and cried as I told God all I had started to say to my husband. Later, in debriefing the experience, my spiritual director pointed out how often I used the term *stuck* or *frozen* when describing my retreat. She offered that I might also have been feeling numb. This word perfectly described my spiritual state on that retreat. For reasons I still do not understand, I spent most of my retreat stuck in a numb, unfeeling layer of my soul. Only afterward, in the safety of my own home, did I break through the spiritual layer of ice and begin to express to God all I could not say, all I did not know I felt on my retreat.

I cannot say, even now, why I was stuck in a numb state during my time away. But I do know that a period of debriefing this experience was what helped me break through, allowing me to glean from what seemed to be wasted time. It is only in hindsight that I saw that God had his own agenda during my retreat, and no matter how I tried to control him, he was not having it. I wanted to battle it out like Jacob and leave with a limp to prove it. I wanted to receive some kind of holy insight and come down the mountain with my face aglow like Moses. But God was doing something different.

God was treating me like Elijah. There were no ravens, but God provided me good food to eat and cozy places to sleep. That was it. Apparently, I was not ready for wrestling or insight. I was only ready for snacks and naps.

In many ways, this first difficult experience has framed how I now approach all retreats: God has his own agenda. The time away is his, and just because I do not understand what he is doing at the time does not mean he is silent or dormant. It has also framed how I return from retreats. Reentry into my "normal" life from a retreat, especially longer retreats, deserves its own time. As much as possible, I try to add in a buffer day or two for reentry, since I've noticed upon return, I am tempted to immediately start deep cleaning my shower grout. Instead I try to leave the second half of the day to retain the slowness I practiced on retreat. It is often an act of effort to continue to rest in my body when I return home, but keeping a slow pace allows what God did on retreat to keep soaking in beneath my soul's surface.

Reentry must be gentle. Think of retreating like the practice of fasting; it must be broken with care or your insides will revolt. Finding time to metabolize what happened on retreat within the first day is usually helpful. I try to add in time after I've left the retreat center and before I get home, to build in some kind of middle space to process and recalibrate. This often looks like a stop on the way home at a coffee shop to write up or otherwise process my thoughts. If this option isn't available—say, you are being towed down a mountain against your will, debrief before you go to bed that night.

So much of our lives is spent going and doing, we do not naturally build in reflection time, yet throughout Scripture, we see the importance of reflecting and remembering. God invites his people continuously to "remember" (Deut 8:1-3). We must remember what God has done, and in the remembering, perhaps make sense of how he works and moves. Reflecting on our experiences is a vital ingredient in our spiritual formation. Without it we keep barreling ahead in life, unable and unwilling to learn from the past. I once heard Trevor Hudson say, "We do not learn from our experiences, we learn from reflecting upon our experiences." Within the first week of returning home, answer the debrief questions in preparation for meeting with your spiritual director, pastor, or friend. Writing down your answers to these questions helps you not only make sense of your retreat experience but also to reflect on the broader rhythm of rest in your life.

We come away to experience face-to-face time with God, and we are often shocked to find that part of the invitation is to see what is in our hearts, as well. How we respond to this experience gives us a good deal of information about ourselves. In retreat, God often allows us to experience our need for him more clearly, but it does not immediately feel this way. We may feel weary and weak, depleted, aimless, and helpless. We might see our failures and flaws and feel deeply disoriented by all that is coming up. We may feel full of shame and self-condemnation. We might feel disoriented by a lack of consolation or good feelings about ourselves or God. We may feel completely numb and detached from God entirely. We can either cooperate with this illumination and what it reveals, or we can resist it and go into any number of tactics to reduce its impact on our experience.

For much of Christian history, believers have understood these feelings of spiritual poverty as important markers on the journey toward spiritual maturity. Saint John of the Cross believed that Christians make "even greater progress" in the dark, when the consolation of good feelings, of peace, of rightness, of joy, is removed. He says, "The soul makes greater progress when it least thinks so, yea, most frequently when it imagines that it is losing." The feelings that Saint John describes become highlighted in extended periods of time when we are invited to examine the state of our souls and find them wanting. He goes on,

> Some of these beginners, too, make little of their faults, and at other times, become over-sad when they see themselves fall into them, thinking themselves to have been saints already; and thus they become angry and impatient with themselves.... Often they beseech God, with great yearnings, that He will take from them their imperfections and faults, but they do this that they may find themselves at peace, and may not be troubled by them, rather than for God's sake; not realizing that, if He should take their imperfections from them, they would become prouder and more presumptuous still.

Saint John aptly names what so many of us experience on retreat: ourselves. Our first response is often to try to rid ourselves of negative feelings as quickly as possible. We do not see the gift of revelation, that God has wooed us out into the wilderness to show us what is in our hearts. We simply want good feelings, not necessarily an encounter with God. It shows us that we have wanted the gifts over the giver, that we wanted peace, joy, satisfaction, and consolation more than we wanted God himself. We might be content with the lesser emotive experiences found in consolation, but God is never content until he has given us himself.

Whether we have an overinflated sense of spiritual sainthood or a deep sense of our own weakness on retreat, God offers to recalibrate our hearts with his presence. We come to see that our retreat is not defined by how we experience it. Many want a "meaningful" retreat; an experience that makes us feel good about ourselves and our spirituality. That's fine and normal, but from what I have seen, often it is not the journey God wants to take us on. People often want to "get better" at prayer, Bible reading, and spirituality in general, but Jesus is simply not interested in making you a better version of yourself. Retreat is not a step in the course of self-actualization.

Hungering and thirsting in the wilderness reveals what is in our hearts by showing us our real selves, not the avatar we often portray to the rest of the world. We must really see and look at our real selves, with all the mess. We must see how lost and broken we are. Only then can we allow God to love that real self—for only an actual self can be loved. God wants to feed you the bread of life on your retreat, not give you better feelings about yourself. To receive this you may need to relinquish your lesser desires for consolation and accept what God has for you.

God uses a lack of felt experience, or darkness and desolation, to purge us of our taste for lesser things. Only then will we truly hunger and thirst for God. Saint John says, "This is the first and principal benefit caused by this arid and dark night of contemplation: the knowledge of oneself and one's misery." As Deuteronomy 8:1-3 shows, first God leads us into wild places, then tests our hearts, then offers knowledge of what lies within, then humility of spirit, then hunger (for the better thing), then satisfaction—a kind only God himself can give.

A time of thoughtful debriefing, especially with another person, is one of the best ways to understand what God is doing in your life. I've found that remembering solidifies, gives needed language, and builds a framework for our brains to understand what is happening. It's like a stitch in fabric. If you start sewing and keep going, the whole beginning of the line will eventually unravel. You must first start with a back stitch, a reinforcing stitch, a return to what was to solidify what is. Then what God is weaving together in your life can hold.

12

QUESTIONS FOR DEBRIEFING

✝

There is a voice that might ask us to measure the "usefulness" of our retreat experience. It asks, "Was this worth it?" "Did I get anything out of it?" "How was this productive or useful?" On retreat it is important to quiet those voices and attend to the simple nature of abiding, of trusting that God is working even in the dark and even if we cannot see it. But here in our debrief time, we can ask some deeper questions and hopefully gain some clarity about what God was actually doing on retreat even if it seemed like nothing was happening at the time.

In Paul's letter to the Galatians, he uses the phrase "until Christ is formed in you" (Gal 4:19) to illustrate maturity in Christ. We may want to grow spiritually and see retreating as a viable path to such growth, but we can never focus on growth for growth's sake. If we seek spiritual growth for its own sake, we will always be seeking inward: *How am I doing, how am I feeling, how much did I pray/read/meditate; how good am I?* Spiritual growth is not the telos; it is not an end for its own sake. For followers of Jesus, *he* is our only telos, our only goal. So Paul uses this language of Christ being formed in us, an image of the person of Christ taking over more and more of us, shaping our capacities, our thoughts, and the focus of our internal world. When we debrief a retreat, it is not helpful to evaluate it in a critical sense, asking what we got out of it or if we feel more spiritually mature or attuned. The main question is: How was Christ formed in me on retreat?

To help deepen your awareness of Christ's formation in you, use these questions as journaling prompts after your retreat to aid in debriefing with a spiritual director, pastor, or trusted friend.

Adele Ahlberg Calhoun says, "Keeping company with Jesus in the space between wanting to change and not being able to change through effort alone can be a difficult thing to do. Desiring God and not demanding an outcome keeps us in the risky place of waiting and longing. The truth is that we do not know how God intends to conform us to the image of his Son."

1. Did you spend time on your retreat in the "risky place of waiting and longing"? If so, were you able to cooperate with God and linger in that space? What helped you stay there? What conspired to move you away from it?

2. Do you see any areas where you were more conformed to the image of Jesus during your time away? How was Christ formed in you on retreat?

3. What themes did you notice on your retreat?

4. What threads can you begin to label and name?

5. Record any Scriptures that God used to speak into your life.

6. In what areas of yourself did you notice a need for deeper healing or restoration (spiritually, mentally, physically, relationally)? What do you think God was doing there? What are your next steps on the path of healing?

7. If you felt numb, detached, or resistant during any part of your retreat, pay special attention to those times and record them. Do any themes emerge?

8. Were there times when you found yourself bored while on retreat? When? What did you do with that?

9. What imagery (especially from nature) did God give you on retreat?

10. What activities were you drawn to do on retreat (reading, writing, journaling, napping, walking, eating, staring off into space for hours, painting with watercolors, bird watching)? What was life-giving to you?

11. What would you like to do differently for your next retreat? What would you keep the same?

12. What surprised you on retreat?

13. Looking back on your retreat, what would you say God was doing?

14. Do you feel as if you were able to participate in what God was doing, or were you trying to make something happen on your own? Or put differently, how did you *cooperate* with Christ being formed in you?

13

COMING AWAY AND COMMUNITY

✝

And [Jesus] went up on the mountain and called to him those whom he desired, and they came to him . . . so that they might be with him and he might send them out.

MARK 3:13-14

Mountains in Scripture symbolize a meeting place with God. From Sinai in Exodus to the Sermon on the Mount in the Gospels to Zion in Revelation, God calls his people to come away to be with him where he is. When we accept the invitation to come away, we are met face-to-face with the living God, who looks on us in love. We join him on the mountain (or the hotel room, or backhouse, or cabin in the forest) and, from that vantage point, more clearly see him for who he is and begin to get a glimpse of ourselves through his eyes. Only from seeing him as he is can we see ourselves for who we are. And from this place, we begin to envision where, when, and how he might send us out.

If we neglect coming away with God, we risk missing this view and are left to fumble around in the dark for life's purpose and meaning. Many try to conjure it up themselves, taking a best guess, throwing darts at the wall hoping somehow to find the bull's-eye. This can lead to living panicked, anxious, harried, and hurried lives, thinking the more activity we do, the more likely it is that we will find that elusive center. We miss out not only on *being* with him but also on where and how he might send us out into a broken and hurting world.

When we heed Jesus' call to come away with him, we cultivate the secret place within ourselves where only God can dwell. Isaiah wrote, "I will give you the treasures of darkness and hidden riches of secret places" (Is 45:3 NKJV). Jesus said, "I have food to eat that you know nothing about" (Jn 4:32 NIV) in regard to the satisfying nature of his inner life when the disciples wondered if he had eaten. The secret place within each one of us is filled to the brim, but often we need to go out to desolate places in retreat to mine the riches within.

One pitfall for those returning from a retreat is to treat this spiritual practice as a one-time event, a box they have now checked off on a spiritual to-do list. Many I have seen, even those who would attest to the benefits of coming away with God, often have a hard time integrating a regular rhythm of retreating into their actual lives. Even though their soul longs to come away with God, and they have tasted and seen that it is good, they resist claiming this space in their lives and calendars as worthy. The reasons for this vary. The time or money spent feels like an unneeded extravagance.

The kids' school, sports, or work calendars fill up without our noticing. Maybe time in silence felt unsettling or even painful, and we justify that there are other, more worthy, spiritual practices to give ourselves to. I've noticed within myself and those I lead no shortage of resistance.

When faced with this resistance in my own life, I have found it important to link the practice of secrecy (cultivating this secret, inner place with God) and the practice of being in community (being sent out into the world) as two sides of the same coin. Both of these practices take time and repetition. All the mountain tableaux we find in Scripture are places of community, the inner community we find with God and the outer community we make with others. The Israelites were not freed from slavery one person at a time but as a whole. Jesus spoke to the masses when he gave the Sermon on the Mount. The picture Scripture offers of the end of all things is a table on a mountain, a place of deep communal intimacy, with more seats than we could have imagined (see Is 25:6-10; Lk 14:21-24).

Dietrich Bonhoeffer said, "Let him who cannot be alone beware of community.... Let him who is not in community beware of being alone." Just as Jesus was fed in the secret, inner places, we, too, have a deep need for secret communion with God. It is no coincidence that in the practice of the Eucharist (or Communion), we gather together to pass the bread of his body among us. "Man shall not live by bread alone," Jesus retorted to the devil in the desert, "but by every word that comes from the mouth of God" (Mt 4:4). We do not eat once. We cannot survive on monthly or even weekly bread, so he told us to ask for it daily, in our bedrooms and closets. We ask for it in solitude "and your Father who sees in secret will reward you" (Mt 6:6). If we are not fed in the secret places, we cannot bring food to those around us. Our secret, inner lives, or lack thereof, have far-reaching implications for the community of the kingdom of God.

The practice of retreating, of going with God into the secret place within ourselves, enlarges our capacity and solidifies that space. If we do not cultivate this place by spending time there, that space remains too small to hold another person. We may *be* with people in community, but because our interior space is so small, it can only hold ourselves: our concerns, our needs, our wants. We are in a community but not intentionally present in a way that helps other people grow.

God is doing a work within you on retreat that may only become apparent after practicing retreating for some time. What I have seen, within myself and others, is that the more we learn to make our home in God, the larger and more beautiful that home grows, making space for others. The more often we retreat to our closets (or cabins, or monasteries), the more readily we engage with others, not less. If our inner life of secrecy is flourishing, then we can engage in a broken world with our broken selves. If we are fed secretly with bread no one knows about, then we are already full when we come to the community table. We want to hear instead of being desperate to be heard. We can be free to minister because we have already been ministered to in secret places.

Training ourselves in the spiritual practice of retreating counteracts the worldly training of our souls. The world's training always aims to make us engines of consumption of both God and neighbor, demanding more from everyone around us, and even of ourselves. Productivity, not love, becomes our metric and currency. People become bodies to further our cause and do our bidding, not beloved brothers and sisters. It dims our eyes to the needs of the community around us, as other people become simply a means to get our personal needs met.

All forms of rest, retreating included, retrain our souls, reminding us we already have all we need. We do not need to be more, to have more, or to get more. All forms of training take time, and one experience is not enough. We must repeatedly taste and see that rest is good for us, and then the natural next step is to see how good it might be for those around us, especially the exploited within our communities. Walter Brueggemann says, "Rest as did the creator God! And while you rest, be sure that your neighbors rest alongside you. Indeed, sponsor a *system of rest* that contradicts the *system of anxiety* of Pharoah."

A. W. Tozer explains the inextricable link between the practices of secrecy and community. In *The Pursuit of God* he says that the members of a church, each attuned privately to the Spirit, come together corporately, naturally in unity, like one hundred pianos all tuned by the same fork. He says the choice is not to focus either on a private or a corporate spirituality but that "social religion is perfected when private religion is purified. The body becomes stronger as its members become healthier. The whole Church of God gains when the members that compose it begin to seek a better and a higher life."

The church was designed to be the hub of the community. We meet together, ignited first by the Spirit and further energized by each other, and then we *go out*. The church, like the individuals who embody it, cannot stay put. Stagnancy is never a kingdom reality, so we must go out . . . together. Our communities desperately need our churches, with healthy and rightly tuned members, active, energized, and engaged within them. Phrased plainly: Committing to a rhythm of retreating is good not only for yourself but also for your community.

When we enter retreat, we consent to come face-to-face with that smoking mountain, that "thick darkness" (Ex 20:21), knowing it is often the only way to meet the living God. We come to find that it is only in entering that darkness that we can engage with the darkness in the lives of those around us. When we rest we "remember" our former status as slaves (Deut 5:15). We recall our lives before the invading presence of God in our midst. Back then we had to work unceasingly because we were trying to make meaning out of our lives. But now we receive our meaning, our purpose, our very personhood from him. And the beautiful invitation to enter into retreat lies here: only free people are allowed to rest. Rest is not an option for slaves, whose lives are dictated by those in power above them. We are no longer slaves, we are free, beloved children of God, invited to come away and rest.

ACKNOWLEDGMENTS

Writing a book was not unlike having a baby. I had an amazing support system that took these words from their incubation in the dark and helped birth them into the world.

Cindy Bunch, you are a true midwife if I ever met one. Thank you for taking a chance on me and guiding both me and this project with wisdom and precision. Rachel O'Connor, Lori Neff, Sheila Urban, and the rest of the team at InterVarsity Press, thank you for treating my words as tenderly as I did and attending to them with care.

I have been blessed with wise and generous teachers in my community at the Institute for Spiritual Formation. Dr. Betsy Barber, Dr. John Coe, Dr. Judy TenElshof, and Dr. Kyle Strobel, I am grateful for the ways you shepherded my soul toward true rest. Your lectures, office hours, feedback, and friendship shaped every page of this book. Chris Baker, you are a champion and guide. Larry Warner, you spoke hope in a difficult season and pushed me to keep writing. To my directees and students, thank you for opening your lives and hearts to me; I couldn't wait to get this book into your hands. To my coworkers and friends, it is my joy to be a link in the chain beside you in the good work God has given us to do.

I am indebted to many doulas who read early versions of this work as it was still taking shape: Angie, Ali, Diana, Andrea, Amy, and countless others. My heart holds so many interactions where a text, prayer, or simple, "How's the book going?" gave me a shot in the arm when I needed it most. Mike Liaw and Carlos Delgado, you were the first professionals to read my work and were gracious beyond measure. Dr. Eddie Gamarra, you made invaluable contributions to my contract. The members of the Redbud Writers Guild offered a community that sustained me in barren seasons. Leeba, you taught me how to pay it forward. Megan, Brit, Brooke, Erin, Tiana, your unwavering encouragement kept me going in the darkest hours.

I'm grateful to my family, who celebrated every small milestone along the way: my family of origin, who instilled an early love of reading, and my inherited family, who walk beside me (and likely bought cases of this book). My kids: Jeremiah, Finn, Claire, Fiona, and Harden, you have been my best spiritual teachers. I never wrote a word worth reading before I birthed you into the world, so every word I write belongs to you. Drew, you made this book a possibility by replacing me as both mother and father so I could come away with Jesus and discover my love of retreats. You never lost hope, even when I did, that these words might see the light of day.

My greatest thanks are reserved for God Almighty, who loved me into rest, who wastes nothing, and who will never let my words fall to the ground.

Appendix A

COMPANIONING:
A GUIDE FOR LEADERS

Note: Many of the questions below were taken from or influenced by the lectures of Dr. Betsy Barber, professor emeritus of Biola University. They are used here with her gracious permission and my grateful acknowledgment.

Five hundred years ago, Saint Ignatius of Loyola initiated into the church an idea of purposeful retreating wherein he developed and led retreatants through his Spiritual Exercises. "The retreat movement began originally as a one-to-one experience, one director and one retreatant. But as time passed and the movement became more popular, people began to make retreats annually, not just once or twice in a lifetime. . . . The ideal one-to-one situation became more and more impractical." In light of this impracticality, the church developed group preached retreats, an approach that naturally led to a depersonalized focus on content and where consumption of information trumped restful time away with the lover of our souls. Over time, the spiritual director evolved into a speaker, unable to meet with retreatants personally to take stock of the individual needs of their souls. Eventually, "the director became a lecturer rather than a co-discerner, and the retreatant was left to face the Lord (and the evil spirit) alone."

Whenever we lead someone through a retreat, we are recapturing a bit of Ignatius's vision to companion with another as they seek the Lord. The focus here is on discerning their personal experiences with God. Our job is to hold the steady presence of God's love, continually pointing them in his direction. We try to notice places where they are face-to-face with themselves and not face-to-face with God, places where they are functioning out of guilt, shame, or their own conscience rather than guided by the Holy Spirit. A retreat is often a microcosm of a larger body of work God is doing in someone's life, so it needs to be treated with great care. It is a vital part of their story with God. I ask questions and take note of how God has spoken to them before. I am not a character in their story, yet I can help them locate God on the pages of their lives.

Retreats by nature are disrupting and disorienting. Our thoughtful questions and reflections, along with the practices in this book, help them name some internal realities that reorient their souls. Often, the best thing we can offer when we accompany someone through a retreat experience is our peaceful presence amid their own darkness, confusion, or apathy. Do not lead people through retreats without proper training and having a regular and robust history of your own retreat experiences to draw on. You cannot take others places you have not traveled yourself.

Ideally, you will accompany someone through a retreat with whom you have an ongoing relationship. At the very least, two meetings are needed—one before their retreat and one after as an element of their debrief. For the questions that follow, do not feel obligated to check them all off your list. This is just a broad framework to guide your discussion. Use discernment on which questions might be most helpful for this particular person.

BEFORE

Before their retreat, set a time to meet with the retreatant to get a feel for where God is already moving in their life and where he might be taking them. You are listening for clues of what kinds of conversations they are having with God, where they are leaning in, and where they might be resisting.

This may be a person you see monthly for a spiritual direction, or a congregant in your church who reached out for guidance. Either way, set aside about an hour to ask questions and hear about their hopes and fears for their retreat. Encourage them to engage with the "Preparation Guide" and "Preparing Your Soul" (chapters three and four) prior to your meeting, if they have not already.

As you attend to them, listen with one ear on the person before you and one ear on the Holy Spirit. Ask God for guidance on how and if to respond.

Practical concerns. Ask the retreatant to walk you through their retreat plan. Who will care for work and family duties while they are away? Are they committed to unplugging from these commitments—phone and all? (Note: having them overtly state their intention here is often helpful for them to recall later when they are tempted to check in on what's going on back home.) What is in place in case of an emergency?

Have they decided to retreat in solitude or with a prayerful community? What led them to make this choice? If food is not provided on-site, how will they procure food? When and how will they get there? Be sure to walk through tangible needs on retreat, especially if there are extenuating circumstances or physical limitations. Pay attention to any places of anxiety or resistance. Where does this come from? How might God be working in this?

As they envision what they would like out of their retreat, help them to consider their specific life stage. Are they behind a desk all day and in need of recreation time? Are they isolated and alone most of the time? What is their body telling them it needs during their time away?

Spiritual concerns. Can the retreatant identify any areas where God is working in their life? (What Scriptures, imagery, songs, or words stand out or are repeated?)

Is there a sense of God adding or removing things in this stage of life?

How is their mind currently "being transformed"? Are there any areas shifting or changing?

How have they been hearing God's voice, or experiencing his presence, if at all?

Who is God to them in this season (Father, Friend, Good Shepherd, Rock, Shelter, Hiding Place, Defender, Deliverer, etc.)?

Have they settled on which retreat to do? Do any of the retreat themes scare or repel them? What made them choose the retreat they did? What stands out to you about that?

What are they hoping for spiritually from this retreat experience? What does their soul need in this season of life?

Mental health concerns. How do they know now is the time to come away with the Lord? Is there a sense of escapism or running away from life's problems? Do they have a history of mental health issues or self-harm? If so, encourage them to get clearance from their doctor or therapist before committing to extended time in solitude. If something comes up during their time away, such as a panic attack, what is their plan? Do they need to give more thought to how to care for their mental health during their time away?

What is the pace of their life as they prepare to enter retreat? Is there a sense that it is unsustainable as is? What might be some ways to ease into silence and solitude?

Are they afraid of any emotions coming up during their time away?

While listening to their responses to these questions, along with how they processed the preparatory questions, ask the Holy Spirit to illuminate any threads or themes this person is experiencing. Pay attention to repeated words and imagery. Ask God for wisdom as to how he is working in this person's life. Pay careful attention to phrases like, "I know God is . . . but I feel . . ." Listen for disconnects between their God image and God concept. Offer compassion and pray about gently reflecting anything you heard back to them. If you offer any insight, do so tentatively, knowing they are the authority on their experience with God.

Prayer. Pray for the retreatant, blessing them on their time away. As you hold their worries, concerns, and hopes before the Lord, ask for the Holy Spirit's guidance in reflecting back what they have shared, including what they are looking forward to on the retreat as well as areas of apprehension. Entrust them to God's care, and assure them of your prayers during their time away.

Follow-up. Schedule your debriefing appointment for a week or two after they have returned and have had time to engage with the questions for debriefing (chapter twelve). Be sure to point out that the longer they are away on retreat, the more significant reentry becomes.

DURING

Next, pray for them during their retreat (this might be the most important). It has brought me great comfort in times of solitude with God to know someone was praying on my behalf. Prayers for those in our care are some of the most powerful words we can offer. Make a note in your calendar for their departure date, and send them a quick email or text to let them know they can count on your prayers. Commit to holding them in prayer during their time away.

AFTER

After they return, meet up again to debrief their experience. Try to do this after they have been able to engage with the debrief questions (chapter twelve), ideally within a few weeks of their return. As you go through these questions, be aware of the very normal temptation to try to manufacture an experience. Try to temper that with compassion.

Pick a few of these questions to explore in your time together:

1. What had you expected or intended and what did you actually experience during your time away?

2. Where were you able to cooperate with God in what he was doing? Where were you not?

3. What has your prayer life been like since returning?

4. Where did you find beauty on your retreat?

5. What were your wishes or desires on retreat? Could you and did you express those to God?

6. What was reentry like for you?

7. Have you expressed what you need with God now that you are back?

8. How did you sleep on retreat?

9. What was your body experiencing on retreat?

10. When did you feel bored, irritable, distracted, or numb? How did you respond?

11. Who was God to you on this retreat?

12. Was it easy or hard psychologically for you to be in solitude? How might that influence your retreat plan going forward?

13. Could you give God your full attention, or did you find yourself overwhelmed with your own sense of self?

14. Where did you notice yourself enjoying God?

15. Were you able to practice holy dawdling?

16. Retreat offers a different vantage point than our daily lives allow. What did God show you on retreat that you might not have been able to see during a normal day?

17. Were there any particularly life-giving aspects of your retreat that you might consider building into your weekly sabbath time?

18. Is there anything from your retreat you need to hold on to or let go of?

19. Was there something that was opened up that you need to stay open to? What will help you stay open to those things?

Some of these questions are easy: "How did you sleep on retreat?" Some are more difficult: "Who was God to you on this retreat?" Be especially gentle if much feels hidden or foggy to the retreatant. It can feel like an act of aggression to have someone ask "Who was God to you?" when you have absolutely no idea who God was to you nor what God was doing on your retreat. This is a time to offer compassion and support. Many people are verbal processors, so they may be realizing things for the first time in their session with you that did not occur to them before. Move slowly here, allowing them to glean all they can by hearing themselves reflect on their experience. It is often difficult to make sense of our experiences with God, and retreatants may look to you to make sense of their experience. Be prayerful about how to respond, if at all. In this time you are looking for overall themes and dynamics of their retreat. Ask God to illuminate anything he wants you to see, and again, offer any reflections you might have tentatively.

Be sure to pray for and bless the retreatant as part of the debrief session. There are so few spaces where we can bare our soul's reality to another person. Their willingness to share their retreat experience with you is an intense honor and privilege. In your responses, try to cast a wider vision of how God might be calling them into a regular schedule of rest as part of their rhythm of life. Even if much feels unclear for the retreatant, we can be a steady anchor, reminding them of God's truth—that he is always calling his beloveds away to be with him where he is.

Appendix B

FURTHER READING FOR THE PRACTICE OF RETREAT

Ruth Haley Barton, *Invitation to Retreat: The Gift and Necessity of Time Away with God*

Ruth Haley Barton, *Embracing Rhythms of Work and Rest: From Sabbath to Sabbatical and Back Again*

Richard J. Foster, *Sanctuary of the Soul: Journey into Meditative Prayer*

Thomas H. Green, *A Vacation with the Lord: A Personal, Directed Retreat based on the Spiritual Exercises of Saint Ignatius*

Thomas H. Green, *Opening to God: A Guide to Prayer*

Emilie Griffin, *Wilderness Time: A Guide for Spiritual Retreat*

Abraham Joshua Heschel, *The Sabbath*

Ben Campbell Johnson and Paul H. Lang, *Time Away: A Guide for Personal Retreat*

Sybil MacBeth, *Praying in Color: Drawing a New Path to God*

Wayne Muller, *Sabbath: Finding Rest, Renewal, and Delight in Our Busy Lives*

Christine Valters Paintner, *The Artist's Rule: Nurturing Your Creative Soul with Monastic Wisdom*

Sue Pickering, *On Holiday With God: Making Your Own Retreat—A Companion and Guide*

Jane Rubietta, *Quiet Places: A Woman's Guide to Personal Retreat*

Phyllis Tickle, *The Divine Hours*

Marjorie J. Thompson, *Soul Feast: An Invitation to the Christian Spiritual Life*

Macrina Wiederkehr, *The Song of the Seed: A Monastic Way of Tending the Soul*

Dallas Willard, *Hearing God: Developing a Conversational Relationship with God*

NOTES

1. THE INVITATION

3   *"The result of our thinginess"*: Abraham Joshua Heschel, *Sabbath* (Farrar, Straus and Giroux, 1951), 1.

9   *"What comes into our minds"*: A. W. Tozer, *The Knowledge of The Holy: The Attributes of God: Their Meaning in the Christian Life* (HarperOne, 2009), chap. 1.

10   *"Dissolves the artificial urgency"*: Wayne Muller, *Sabbath: Restoring the Sacred Rhythm of Rest* (Bantam, 2000), 83.

12   *"When it is evening"*: Eugene Peterson, "Rhythms of Grace," *Weavings* 8, no. 2 (March–April 1993): 16, as quoted in Marjorie J. Thompson, *Soul Feast: An Invitation to the Christian Spiritual Life* (Westminster John Knox Press, 2014), 72.

2. THE ELEMENTS

18   *We "pull back from the battle line"*: Ruth Haley Barton, *Invitation to Retreat: The Gift and Necessity of Time Away with God* (InterVarsity Press, 2018), 11.

19   *"Our culture supposes"*: Wayne Muller, *Sabbath: Finding Rest, Renewal and Delight in Our Busy Lives* (Random House, 2000), 1.

22   *The word* prayer *in Aramaic*: Rocco A. Errico, *Setting a Trap for God: The Aramaic Prayer of Jesus* (Unity Books, 1997), as quoted by Northumbria Community, *Celtic Daily Prayer Book One* (William Collins Publishing, 2001), 7.

25   *Their passion for the Word*: Thomas Cahill, *How the Irish Saved Civilization: The Untold Story of Ireland's Heroic Role from the Fall of Rome to the Rise of Medieval Europe* (Doubleday, 1995).

26   *"Our task"*: Marjorie J. Thompson, *Soul Feast: An Invitation to the Christian Spiritual Life* (John Knox Press, 1995), 21.
    "With the ear of our heart": Dallas Willard, *Hearing God: Developing a Conversational Relationship with God* (InterVarsity Press, spec. ed., 2012), 50.

27   *"Encountering God himself"*: Willard, *Hearing God*, 44.

29   *We move from "communicating with God"*: Thompson, *Soul Feast*, 44.

30   *"Monasteries sanctify time"*: Gerald L. Sittser, *Water from a Deep Well: Christian Spirituality from Early Martyrs to Modern Missionaries* (InterVarsity Press, 2010), 97.

31   *"Such routine creates"*: Sittser, *Water from a Deep Well*, 115.

38   *"Sheep will only lie down"*: Kenneth Bailey, *The Good Shepherd: A Thousand-Year Journey from Psalm 23 to the New Testament* (IVP Academic, 2014), 40.

      "The shepherd knows": Bailey, *The Good Shepherd*, 23.

41   *"Since our enslavement occurs"*: Emilie Griffin, *Wilderness Time: A Guide for Spiritual Retreat* (HarperOne, 1997), 21.

43   *Free writing for fifteen to twenty minutes*: James Pennebaker, *Opening Up by Writing It Down: How Expressive Writing Improves Health and Eases Emotional Pain*, 3rd ed. (Guildford Press; 2016).

      "Prayer is not a place": Kyle Strobel and John Coe, *Where Prayer Becomes Real: How Honesty with God Transforms Your Soul* (Baker Books, 2021).

3. PREPARATION GUIDE

46   *"The trick, of course"*: Eugene H. Peterson, *The Contemplative Pastor: Returning to the Art of Spiritual Direction* (Eerdmans, 1993).

47   *"Grace is not opposed"*: Dallas Willard, *The Great Omission: Reclaiming Jesus's Essential Teachings on Discipleship* (HarperOne, 2014).

6. FOR ONE IN NEED OF REST

63   *Attention is treated as a resource*: Matthew B. Crawford, introduction to *The World Beyond Your Head: On Becoming an Individual in an Age of Distraction* (Farrar, Straus and Giroux, 2015), 11.

      In an information-rich world: Herbert A. Simon, "Designing Organizations for an Information-Rich World," *International Library of Critical Writings in Economics* 70: 187-202.

64   *"Tyranny of the urgent"*: Charles E. Hummel, *Tyranny of the Urgent* (InterVarsity Press, 1994).

67   *"Their attachments"*: Thomas H. Green, *Weeds Among the Wheat: Discernment, Where Prayer and Action Meet* (Ave Maria Press, 1984).

73   *"How does this connect"*: Dallas Willard, *Hearing God: Developing a Conversational Relationship with God*, spec. ed. (InterVarsity Press, 2012), 50-51.

77   *"Their attachments"*: Green, *Weeds Among the Wheat*.

83   *"How does this connect?"*: Willard, *Hearing God*, 50-51.

86   *Prayer of Recollection*: Structure and some content adapted from "Prayer of Recollection" by Dr. John H. Coe, Talbot School of Theology. Biola University.

91   *menō*: James Strong, *Strong's Expanded Exhaustive Concordance of the Bible* (Thomas Nelson, 2001), in Greek Lexicon under *menō* #3306.

94   *"Their attachments"*: Green, *Weeds Among the Wheat*.

101 *"Listen to your life"*: Frederick Buechner, *Now and Then: A Memoir of Vocation* (HarperOne, 1991).

106 *"How does this connect"*: Willard, *Hearing God*, 50-51.

107 *"Holy Scripture cries aloud!"*: Saint Benedict, *Rule of Saint Benedict*, AD 530, chap. 7.

     The "word 'obedience'": Esther de Waal, *Seeking God: The Way of St. Benedict* (The Liturgical Press, 2001), 43.

7. FOR ONE WHO IS WEARY

118 *"Dark emotions don't go away"*: Miriam Greenspan, *Healing Through the Dark Emotions: The Wisdom of Grief, Fear and Despair* (Shambhala, 2004).

     Spiritual bypassing: A phrase first coined in 1984 by psychologist John Welwood referring to the tendency to avoid dark or unresolved emotions by suppressing them with spiritual realities of any faith tradition.

119 *Earliest Christians understood*: Saint John of the Cross, *Dark Night of the Soul* (Dover Publications, 2003).

135 *"Despair prayer"*: Sybil MacBeth, *Praying in Color: Drawing a New Path to God* (Paraclete Press, 2009).

142 *"Serenity Prayer"*: "The Full Serenity Prayer (Long Version)," Sober Speak, April 18, 2022, https://soberspeak.com/the-long-version-of-the-serenity-prayer/.

8. FOR A TIME OF TRANSITION

147 *"Transition(s) of the heart"*: Gordon T. Smith, *Courage and Calling: Embracing Your God-Given Potential* (InterVarsity Press, 2011), 15.

149 *"Earth's crammed with heaven"*: Elizabeth Barrett Browning, *Aurora Leigh*, 1856.

150 *"How does this connect"*: Dallas Willard, *Hearing God: Developing a Conversational Relationship with God*, spec. ed. (InterVarsity Press, 2012), 50-51.

156 *"The soul is like"*: Parker J. Palmer, *Let Your Life Speak: Listening for the Voice of Vocation* (Jossey-Bass, 1999), 7-8.

162   *"Egypt was clear socially"*: Eugene H. Peterson, *Run with the Horses: The Quest for Life at Its Best* (InterVarsity Press, 2009), 192.

9. FOR ONE WHO IS GRIEVING

172   *"The dark emotions"*: Miriam Greenspan, *Healing Through the Dark Emotions: The Wisdom of Grief, Fear and Despair* (Shambhala, 2004), 75.

174   *Walking with Grief*: Andy Raine, "Walking with Grief," in *Celtic Daily Prayer*, vol. 1, *The Journey Begins*, The Northumbria Community Trust (William Collins Publishing, 2015). Used by permission.

177   *"By themselves the Spiritual Disciplines"*: Richard Foster, *Celebration of Discipline: The Path to Spiritual Growth* (HarperOne, 2018), 7.

185   *"It is better to come"*: Tish Harrison Warren, *Prayer in the Night: For Those Who Work or Watch or Weep* (InterVarsity Press, 2021).

189   *"What is true of the body"*: Jerry Sittser, *A Grace Disguised: How the Soul Grows through Loss* (Zondervan, 2021), 50, 49.

191   *"A Blessing as You Go"*: James Bryan Smith, address at the Apprentice Gathering, Sept. 26-28, 2024, Wichita, Kansas.

10. FOR ONE IN NEED OF DISCERNMENT

194   *kataritzō*: James Strong, *Strong's Expanded Exhaustive Concordance of the Bible* (Thomas Nelson, 2001) in Greek Lexicon under *"katartizō,"* definition #2675.

195   *Three "expressions of vocation"*: Gordon T. Smith, *Courage and Calling: Embracing Your God-Given Potential* (InterVarsity Press, 2011), 2.

196   *"The quality of our work"*: Smith, *Courage and Calling*, 35.

197   *"The woman of Proverbs 31"*: Smith, *Courage and Calling*, 29.

199   *"Everyone is invited"*: Smith, *Courage and Calling*, 39.

205   *"How does this connect"*: Dallas Willard, *Hearing God: Developing a Conversational Relationship with God*, spec. ed. (InterVarsity Press, 2012), 50-51.

207   *"Kind of relationship God intends"*: Willard, *Hearing God*, 32.

210   *"It seems significant"*: Marjorie J. Thompson, *Soul Feast: An Invitation to the Christian Spiritual Life* (Westminster John Knox, 2014).

213   *"In many cases"*: Willard, *Hearing God*, 72.

215   *God has created me*: Saint John Henry Newman, *Meditations and Devotions, Part III, Meditations on Christian Doctrine* (Longmans, Green, and Co., 1908), 5, https://play.google.com/books/reader?id=LyRLAQAA MAAJ&pg=GBS.PA2&hl=en.

11. REENTRY

224 *"We do not learn"*: I heard this quote during the Apprentice Gathering, Sept. 26-28, 2024, in Wichita, Kansas. Some attribute this quote to turn-of-the-century educator John Dewey.

225 *"The soul makes greater progress"*: Saint John of the Cross, *Dark Night of the Soul* (Dover Publications, 2003).

226 *"The first and principal benefit"*: Saint John of the Cross, *Dark Night.*

12. QUESTIONS FOR DEBRIEFING

229 *"Keeping company with Jesus"*: Adele Ahlberg Calhoun, *Spiritual Disciplines Handbook: Practices That Transform Us* (InterVarsity Press, 2015), 21.

13. COMING AWAY AND COMMUNITY

233 *"Let him who cannot be alone"*: Dietrich Bonhoeffer, *Life Together: The Classic Exploration of Christian Community* (HarperOne, 2009).

235 *"Rest as did the creator God!"*: Walter Brueggemann, *Sabbath as Resistance: Saying No to the Culture of Now* (Westminster John Knox, 2014), 30, italics in original.
"Social religion is perfected": A. W. Tozer, *The Pursuit of God* (Moody Publishers, 2015).

APPENDIX A

239 *"The retreat movement began"*: Thomas H. Green, *A Vacation with the Lord: A Personal, Directed Retreat* (Ave Maria Press, 1986), 18.
"The director became a lecturer": Green, *A Vacation with the Lord*, 18.

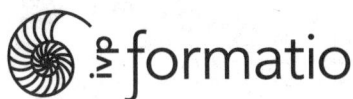

IVP formatio

The nautilus is one of the sea's oldest creatures. Beginning with a tight center, its remarkable growth pattern can be seen in the ever-enlarging chambers that spiral outward. The nautilus in the IVP Formatio logo symbolizes deep inward work of spiritual formation that begins rooted in our souls and then opens to the world as we experience spiritual transformation. The shell takes on a stunning pearlized appearance as it ages and forms in much the same way as the souls of those who devote themselves to spiritual practice. Formatio books draw on the ancient wisdom of the saints and the early church as well as the rich resources of Scripture, applying tradition to the needs of contemporary life and practice.

Within each of us is a longing to be in God's presence. Formatio books call us into our deepest desires and help us to become our true selves in the light of God's grace.

LIKE THIS BOOK?

Scan the code to discover more content like this!

Get on IVP's email list to receive special offers, exclusive book news, and thoughtful content from your favorite authors on topics you care about.

IVPRESS.COM/BOOK-QR